Advance praise for *Beyond Corporate Transformation*

"*Beyond Corporate Transformation* should be read by all who have aspirations of a high performance organization. Christopher Head understands the necessity for holistic change necessary to realize the benefits of higher quality, higher productivity and improved quality of work life. The whole systems approach will allow involved people to revolutionize organizational effectiveness. We have just begun!"

— BILL GARWOOD, RETIRED PRESIDENT
EASTMAN DIVISION, EASTMAN CHEMICAL COMPANY
WINNER, NATIONAL QUALITY AWARD

"Transformation of any company necessarily balances the elimination of outdated systems alongside the preservation of core assets. Christopher Head successfully provides a lucid and coherent guide detailing not only the key elements, but also a sequential approach."

— THOMAS A. GOLUB, PRESIDENT & CEO
HOBBS GROUP, INC.

"In my opinion, any organization that faithfully applies the concepts, practices and recommendations discussed in *Beyond Corporate Transformation* would increase its chances substantially for becoming a more successful entity."

— DAVID K. BALDWIN, PRINCIPAL
BALDWIN & ASSOCIATES
FORMER MALCOLM BALDRIGE QUALITY EXAMINER

"Christopher Head has captured the essence of the challenges of transformation that organizations like ours have faced. Transforming an organization, like health, requires paying attention to the whole system. Chris has captured the key elements of transformation."

"Companies today are trying to take advantage of new information technologies and effectively utilize them for empowering employees. The high performance companies of the 21st century are those that can do this successfully. Christopher Head has identified the critical factors needed for successful transformations and how to sustain them. He has done an excellent job identifying and explaining these success factors in a systems approach. This is a powerful tool for anyone trying to manage toward the 21st century."

BEYOND CORPORATE TRANSFORMATION

BEYOND

CORPORATE

TRANSFORMATION

A Whole Systems Approach to Creating and
Sustaining High Performance

Christopher W. Head

PRODUCTIVITY PRESS
Portland, Oregon

Additional copies of this book are available from the publisher. Discounts are available for multiple copies through the Sales Department (800-394-6868). Address all other inquiries to:

Productivity Press
P.O. Box 13390
Portland, OR 97213-0390
United States of America
Telephone: 503-235-0600
Telefax: 503-235-0909
E-mail: service@ppress.com

Cover and text design by Bill Stanton
Cover photograph by PhotoDisc
Page composition by The Marathon Group, Inc., Durham, North Carolina.
Printed and bound by Edwards Brothers in the United States of America.

Library of Congress Cataloging-in-Publication Data
Head, Christopher W.
    Beyond corporate transformation : a whole systems approach to creating and sustaining high performance / Christopher W. Head.
      p. cm.
    Includes bibliographical references and index.
    ISBN 1-56327-176-1
    1. Organizational change. 2. Organizational effectiveness. I. Title.
HD58.8.H4 1997
658.4'063 — dc21   97-18543
                                                     CIP

02 01 00 99 98 97   10 9 8 7 6 5 4 3 2 1

To my mother and father,
for teaching me the important things in life:
honesty, generosity, and love.

Contents

PART ONE: Preparing for the Transformation

PART TWO: Transforming the Work System

PART THREE: Transforming the Human System/Sustaining the Change Effort

Publisher's Message

Why have so many organizations experienced the upheaval of a change effort only to slip back into the same patterns and habits they were in before? Why do some companies eagerly take the change-effort plunge only to fall short, implementing only a few elements or none at all? In *Beyond Corporate Transformation*, Christopher Head examines the fundamental reasons why some companies succeed while others fail.

To go beyond an ordinary transformation you must have an organizational transformation that encompasses a whole-systems approach to change. Organizational transformation simply means the step-by-step process of reconstructing an existing organization—removing what does not work, keeping that which does, and implementing new systems where appropriate. As a company travels down the change-effort road the roles, rules, and habits in the organization must change on all levels. This creates a lot of chaos, resistance, and stress on its leaders, employees, and processes. Drawing from a wide variety of change methodologies and using interviews conducted at several successful companies, Head goes beyond technical jargon to deal systematically and practically with these difficulties.

In Part One he tackles the critical questions leaders need to answer when undertaking an organizational transformation. Using a seven-stage change management plan, Head shows how leaders can tap into the potential of all employees and empower them by sharing information, decision-making responsibility, and strategic information. This begins the important task of establishing a relationship built on trust and mutual respect between leaders and employees.

Part Two is about redesigning the organization. Head lays out an eight-stage transition team activity plan that has as its central theme, total employee involvement. To Head this means *employees who will be affected by the transformation must effect the changes.* He then details a core process redesign strategy, incorporating all the elements needed to align and link a company's technical systems. Now the organization is ready to push decision-making downward to the employees who are closest to the customers, forming what Head refers to as "natural" work teams. These are teams that have direct responsibility for delivering value to the customers.

In Part Three Head shows leaders how they can empower natural work teams by creating open communication channels, building on existing relationship networks, and eliminating functional barriers. It is in this flatter, leaner environment the traditional career ladders for senior and middle management dissolve. Yet Head shows that by using a "spiral stepcase" approach to careers the forward-looking manager can turn this threatening environment into many new opportunities.

Throughout *Beyond Corporate Transformation* Head uncovers the "musts" that will keep your change effort well oiled and lasting. Most importantly, organizations "must" develop a new performance measurement system that empowers teams to measure, manage, and improve their piece of the process. And behind this measurement system is the "must" for a new performance-based compensation system to reward those teams that deliver increased value to customers. Finally, to sustain a competitive advantage after a change effort, organizations "must" make learning available to all employees with continuous educational and training programs. Only by tapping into the potential of all employees and creating a learning organization will you create a high-involvement organization.

When you finish this book you will see leaders must go beyond incremental changes. They must go beyond reengineering and the limited ideas of change to align the systems, structure, and culture of the whole company. They must go beyond traditional relationships between "thinkers" and "doers" to empower employees to have ownership in the new processes—enabling all employees to excel and execute the company's chosen strategy. Only in this way can a leader be free to focus on what he or she is meant to do—lead and continuously set and recalibrate the direction of the organization. Only then will you have an organizational transformation that works—and continues working.

We are pleased Christopher Head chose Productivity to publish his first book, a book that addresses our on-going concern regarding corporate leadership, corporate change-efforts, and employee involvement. Christopher Head's interests in change management, leadership development, and the transformation of the healthcare industry, as well as his involvement in Miller Howard's Internet-based consulting, research, and electronic library brings valuable insights to all these issues. I like this book and I know you will also.

We wish to thank all those who participated in shaping this manuscript and bringing it to bound book: Diane Asay, editor in chief; Gary Peurasaari for editing the manuscript; James Cole for copyediting; Jane Loftus for proofreading; Mary Junewick for managing the production process; The Marathon Group, Inc. for typesetting; and Bill Stanton for page design and cover design.

Norman Bodek
Chairman

Foreword

When I think back over the years of being involved in leading an organizational transformation, I am amazed at how similar it is to a roller coaster ride. At one moment it seems as though you are at the top of the world, and all is well. You can see everything very clearly. The next moment, the bottom falls out from under you. It happens so fast that you cannot catch your breath. You do not know what lies waiting at the bottom of your fall; and if you survive, what happens next. In the end, if all goes well on the ride, you will complete the fixed course though, at the moment, all of the ups and downs make you oblivious to the full route you are traveling.

In corporate transformations, like the riders on a roller coaster, people are caught up in the events of the moment and do not see the complete ride. Someone must have a planned course for the future. This is what Christopher Head has done for you and me with *Beyond Corporate Transformation: A Whole systems Approach to Creating and Sustaining High Performance*.

There have been numerous times during our transformation at Shell Oil Company that I have pondered questions such as, "What is the next step that makes sense for the organization to take? How fast should we go? Should the present activities take root before proceeding?" These and many other questions must be addressed in the transformation process. Christopher's book does a wonderful job of laying out the various elements of a transformation, as well as describing their applicability. Being aware of the elements gives you the assurance to know what needs to be addressed and when. Having this confidence is so important because when you are in the middle of the implementation process, there will be all sorts of distractions and signs of resistance that will cause you to rethink the process. Staying on course, as Christopher describes, is crucial.

Another important point to make is the universality of the approach. So many times I hear "Yes, but we are different." Yes, the people and situations are different, but the basic processes and elements do apply across various businesses and industries. The specific application, however, does depend upon the particular circumstances of the organization and the appropriate customization does need to be incorporated.

The process Christopher Head defines in *Beyond Corporate Transformation* will get significant, measurable results, both in the near term and in the future. Achieving tangible results is essential to sustaining the energy the orgaanization needs to continue the transformation process.

Christopher has outlined the key levers to initiating and successfully maintaining the transformation effort. I applaud him for this, but also for focusing on implementation. It seems obvious that implementation needs to be addressed, but my experience has been that it is the least understood and most underutilized part of the process, yet it is critical. This book places the appropriate focus on how implementation should be addressed throughout the transformation process.

Christopher has studied the various aspects of our organization's transformation activities. Quite often individuals from other companies who have visited us are looking for the evidence that supports their particular theory of organizational transformation. Christopher did not take that approach. He has impressed me with his objectivity and insights into how all of the pieces fit together and why they work the way they do.

Having these insights from the numerous companies he has studied, combined with his unique ability to not only recognize the key elements of the transformation but to capture their essence in this writing, makes for an excellent book that is well worth reading. Not only is *Beyond Corporate Transformation* worth reading, but it should be your guide to a successful transformation.

May your roller coaster ride be fun and highly rewarding!

Dennis B. Taylor
Manager, Continuous Performance Improvement
Shell Oil Company

Preface

This book describes a process through which corporate leaders can create a high-performance organization capable of sustaining a lasting competitive advantage. It is an approach that takes into consideration all of the factors that affect organizational performance. By examining the whole organization, and by aligning its systems, structure, and culture to enable all employees to excel and execute the company's chosen strategy, corporate leaders can successfully transform their organization.

The transformation process I describe in this book reflects the findings from three years of research that I began in September 1993 as a graduate student at the Georgia Institute of Technology. I set out with the goal of creating a unique and comprehensive change process building on the current management techniques of the day, and learning from progressive companies leading change in their industry. The initial companies I investigated in my study included BellSouth, Rockwell International, The Southern Company, Southland Life, and DeKalb Medical Center. I conducted additional research through interviews with partners and consultants at management consulting firms, including Gemini Consulting, Deloitte & Touche, Andersen Consulting, and Ernst & Young.

Since joining Miller Howard Consulting Group I have had the opportunity to add additional companies to my study through my work with clients such as Shell Oil Company and Coca-Cola de Argentina. This book is the culmination of my research to date; it incorporates insights, experiences, and knowledge from hundreds of leaders, change agents, consultants, managers, employees, and customers in dozens of companies and industries.

Although targeted at corporate leaders, this book will benefit anyone interested or involved in any aspect of organizational change. By understanding the components of organizational change, frontline employees and middle-level managers alike can more effectively participate in and guide the change effort in their part of the organization. A successful organizational transformation is never the sole accomplishment of a leader and his or her senior team. Rather, the transformation is achieved through the hard work and commitment of all types of leaders throughout the entire organization. The following overview outlines the transformation plan this book provides.

Chapter One describes what is meant by the term organizational transformation and examines why companies should consider undergoing a transformation. The fate of companies that accept the status quo is mentioned.

Chapter Two focuses on the role of leadership and on the specific elements that must be in place prior to launching the transformation, with an emphasis on creating a strategic direction, generating top management support, and establishing new cultural values.

Chapter Three explains how leaders can effect change by creating an environment that fosters participation and ownership. It also presents a change management plan that details the activities and actions necessary to manage a successful transformation.

Chapter Four focuses on the elements needed to truly empower employees, with particular emphasis on sharing financial data, decision-making responsibility, and strategic information with employees.

Chapter Five highlights the role employee teams (transition teams) must play in the transformation process. This chapter builds on the principle that the employees who will be affected by the transformation must effect the changes. Anything short of total employee involvement during the transformation effort will increase the likelihood that the changes will not be implemented.

Chapter Six details a core process redesign strategy that incorporates all of the elements needed to successfully transform a company's technical or work systems. Particular emphasis is given to developing a blueprint of the company's redesigned, realigned, and newly linked processes that will deliver increased value to customers.

Chapter Seven reviews how to go about putting "natural" work teams in place as the primary building blocks for organizational performance. At the center of this process is the need to create "good" jobs for all employees. This chapter examines the terms "natural" and "good," as well as the advantages that are realized when teams are well established throughout the organization.

Chapter Eight looks at the structural changes that must be completed to allow the new "natural" work teams to deliver increased value to customers. In particular, this chapter will answer how organizations should go about replacing their traditional hierarchical structures with flatter, more horizontal ones. The changing role of middle and senior management is also discussed.

Chapter Nine examines the importance of developing a new performance measurement system that provides the work teams with the necessary feedback to continually improve their performance. The chapter details principles behind such a new performance measurement system.

Chapter Ten considers the importance of creating a new performance-based compensation system to reward those teams that deliver increased value to customers. Without a system in place to reward high performance, employees will not be significantly motivated to continuously improve their performance.

Chapter Eleven discusses why organizations must make learning available to all of their employees in order to sustain their competitive advantage. It also describes how innovative companies are creating "learning organizations" by developing formal learning systems.

Chapter Twelve summarizes the advantages of using a comprehensive (whole systems) organizational transformation plan and tells why this plan works where other change efforts fall short.

As with any author writing about a complex subject, I have struggled with presenting this transformation strategy in a sequential and linear format, i.e., Chapter 1, followed by Chapter 2, then Chapter 3, and so on. Nonetheless, you must undertake certain transformation phases prior to beginning others for a successful change effort. For this reason I have structured this book in a sequential manner. Wherever it was appropriate I have made links between chapters, and I have indicated when certain processes described in different chapters need to be undertaken simultaneously.

Because of the complexity of organizational change, you must constantly evaluate and reevaluate the success or impact of different parts of the change effort on the overall change strategy. You cannot complete step one or phase one then forget about it as you move on and make changes during the next phase. And because employees always require some degree of stability while undergoing change, some change success factors, such as open and honest communication, trust, and strong leadership, must remain constant throughout. Although these success factors will be detailed in the first few chapters, they will be demanded by employees during every phase of the transformation.

The goal of this book is to provide you with a comprehensive transformation process that will help you change the systems, structure, and culture of your organization. By addressing all of the factors that affect organizational performance you will be creating a high-performance organization capable of sustaining a lasting competitive advantage.

Acknowledgments

An exceptional group of individuals contributed to this book. I am grateful to them for their ideas, insights, and encouragement. In particular, I would like to thank the following consultants for their valuable time and assistance: Jennifer Howard, Lawrence Miller, Michelle Tisdale, and all other members of the Miller Howard Consulting Group, Inc.; Harry Moser of Gemini Consulting; Curtis Songer and several members of the National Reengineering Development Team at Deloitte & Touche LLP; David Pugmire of Andersen Consulting; Jeffrey Busch of Ernst & Young LLP; Dave Baldwin, a Malcolm Baldrige Quality Examiner and Independent Business Consultant; Maxene Raices of Right Associates; and Dory Ingram and Molly Samuels of The Molidori Group.

I also owe thanks to many kind and generous individuals in the business community. In particular: Denny Taylor, Ralph Kerr, Tom Willard, and Paul Lotts of Shell Oil Company; Marvin Dehne of Allina Health System; Dale Register, Jim Satterfield, Dick Franklin, and several additional employees of BellSouth; Furney Powell, Barry Mathis, Don Eckles, Bob Meek, and Larry Coleman of Rockwell International; Becky Wells, Steve Christopher, Buddy Bunn, Nancy Dunaway, Gina Hay, and Pam Gammon of Southland Life; Robin Underwood and Deborah Dale of DeKalb Medical Center; and Anne Marie Ylipahkala of the Southern Company.

On the personal side, I owe special gratitude to my close friend, David Aquino, who provided encouragement, advice, and pages of valuable feedback throughout the creation of this book. Additional thanks go to my brother, John Head, for sharing with me his knowledge of the insurance industry, and to Michael Ulin, for his challenging and thought-provoking questions regarding this book.

Additionally, I thank my editors at Productivity Press, Diane Asay and Gary Peurasaari. Their guidance, strong technical knowledge, and hard work is reflected throughout this book.

Finally, I owe special thanks to Hagood Bellinger, Executive-In-Residence at Georgia Institute of Technology's Graduate School of Management, for his substantive contributions and generous assistance. Hagood has been a source of wisdom and a true mentor. This book would not have been possible without his help and support.

PART ONE

Preparing for the

Transformation

What it Takes to Transform Your Organization

> *"The whole idea of hierarchical management with a general at the top and then several colonels comes out of the military and was transplanted into government as well as into business institutions. This pyramid organization never fit the needs of business, or any other institution."*
>
> —JAMES BURKE [1]
> (FORMER CHAIRMAN OF JOHNSON & JOHNSON)

What Is Going Wrong?

With the abundance of new management concepts and consultant buzzwords flooding corporate America and the business world, it is easy to understand employees' increasing resistance to change. Few companies have been untouched by some type of change effort, whether it be reengineering, downsizing, rightsizing, implementing TQM, ISO 9000, JIT inventory, or some other management or process trend. Organizations throughout the world have spent weeks, months, or in some cases years pursuing and implementing hot new concepts or programs launched by consultants or their own leaders. Their employees have seen it all; and many companies are no better off now than they were before.

Why are so many change efforts failing? Given the complexity of organizational change, no one answer can explain all of the reasons why so many companies fail to realize gains from their change initiatives. Yet, at the same time, common themes have emerged from the hundreds, if not thousands, of organizational change efforts that have failed to reach the goals that were desired.

Common Themes: Why Change Efforts Fail

Of the many themes that have emerged from my research on change efforts, I have identified three core reasons why companies fail to reap the benefits they desire and why they are unable to create and sustain a lasting competitive advantage:

1. Losing sight of those in the organization who are closest to the customer and most important to the success of the change effort—the frontline employee
2. Failing to align and link all business and change activities with the company's strategic direction
3. Failing to establish continuous learning and improvement systems that sustain the gains made during the change effort

If you take a close look at what goes on during many organizational change efforts you will see these themes repeated over and over again, with different variations, by all types of companies. For example, there are companies that keep their employees in the dark about the changes being made around them, yet they expect their employees to "buy into" and support a change effort they know very little about. Other companies hope to create a competitive advantage by launching an endless series of "programs of the month," each different and unlinked, dragging their employees through them month after month, year after year. Still other companies realize positive results from their change efforts, only to watch their competitive advantages fade, because their competitors have systems in place to make learning and advanced training available to all employees and can make process improvements faster.

To realize all of the potential benefits of an organizational change effort, companies need to develop a change process that avoids the pitfalls mentioned above. The organizational transformation process detailed in this book avoids these pitfalls and describes a change process that considers all of the elements that affect organizational performance.

What Is an Organizational Transformation?

The term *organizational transformation* means the step-by-step process of reconstructing an existing organization — removing what does not work, keeping that which does, and implementing new systems, structures, or cultural values where appropriate. No company can install completely new systems, replace its entire workforce, or build all new structures. Even if they could, none would want to. Instead, organizations want to benefit from as many improvements as possible by leaving in place what is still of value, replacing what is broken and out-dated, and redesigning what can be modified.

An organizational transformation is like the reconstruction of a large building. For example, suppose the owners of a 250-unit residential building decide to pursue a strategy of targeting their building toward a more sophisticated and wealthy segment of the market. This might mean modernizing their older building, both in terms of appearance and technology. They also might want to reduce operating expenses by installing new, more efficient systems.

After examining the strengths and weaknesses of the building, they conclude that the building's solid structure, great location, and experienced staff are all valuable assets. Except for plans to offer severance packages to a few employees and to provide additional training, they want to leave these valuable assets untouched. But they decide that the outdated heating and air conditioning, elevator, and security systems all need replacement. New technology will dramatically decrease operating expenses and improve service and security. With the remaining money in the budget they plan to renovate the building's exterior, lobby, and parking area. The cosmetic changes and additional parking spaces will make the building a more attractive and accessible place to live. They plan to involve the residents in the project by informing them of all the changes and listening to any suggestions they might have to offer.

After the renovation and reconstruction, it is still the same basic building, yet it has a better-trained staff and it has improved its image, is more efficient, and is safer for its residents. The residents had to adjust their living arrangements during the year-long renovation, but they were pleased that they were invited to participate in decisions about the building's renovation. They look forward to being involved in future decisions that affect their residence.

After the renovation, the building's property value increases, and it is now attracting wealthier residents and raising the occupancy rate. Operating costs drop, and security problems become almost nonexistent. And although the modernization required a significant investment, both in time and money, the owners recoup their investment in a relatively short period and increase their profit margins. The residents, staff, and owners view the renovation as a huge success.

What It Takes for Organizations to Transform

Albeit more simple than the organizational transformation of any company, the renovation example should help you understand many of the issues that arise during an organizational change effort. With the residential building it is easy to visualize what part of the building remains intact, what part is junked, and what elements are upgraded or modified. It is harder to picture how organizations are transforming themselves, especially companies that generate, transmit, and distribute knowledge. The conceptual picture below will help define a successful transformation, as will the two transformation case studies of Rockwell International and Asea Brown Boveri.

Organizations realize a successful transformation when they tap into the potential of all employees and align the systems, structure, and culture with the strategy of the organization. In this high-involvement, high-performance organization, employees of all levels throughout the organization are given information, more power, and decision-making responsibilities, which allow middle and senior managers to focus on long-term strategic issues. A new culture is formed, one based on trust, open communication, and continuous learning. Processes are redesigned to radically improve customer service, reduce cost, and respond quickly to business opportunities and threats. In addition, these successful organizations establish work teams that experience *ownership* of a process or sub-process. A flat organizational structure replaces the steep managerial hierarchy that directed all *thinking* upward and all *doing* downward. Measurement systems are redesigned to give direct and immediate customer feedback to those teams that need the information to adjust or correct their processes. Compensation is tied into individual, team, and company performance giving employees a financial stake in the organization. Finally, the organization fosters continuous learning and training to maintain and improve their performance. This is what it will take to transform your organization, to create and *sustain* a competitive advantage. Challenging? Yes. Impossible? No.

Whether you label the change effort an organizational transformation, or reengineering, or right-sizing, or quality-building effort, a common language should be established inside the company, and the focus should be on the principles or values behind the change effort—what you are changing and what are the bottom-line outcomes. While the principles or values may be worded differently from company to company, the underlying goal should always be to utilize the potential of all employees. This is the only true way to create an organization in which every employee can add value to the customers. As for what a company is changing, successful transformations dramatically improve their structure, process, and culture. Only when these three elements are aligned and working in harmony can employees reach their true potential, a potential that will in turn add the greatest value to the company and to its customers.

Companies That Have Successfully Transformed

Most importantly, a change effort should be judged on its bottom-line outcomes. A value-oriented, employee-focused change effort that produces little or no financial benefit is a waste of time. This type of outcome may temporarily boost morale and employee satisfaction, but if it fails to translate into financial gains then the effort was unsuccessful. The following two examples will highlight a successful organization transformation.

ROCKWELL INTERNATIONAL — TACTICAL SYSTEMS DIVISION. When the leadership team at Rockwell International launched the transformation of the company, they had the goal of changing from a company that "got the product out the door at all costs" to one that "does things right the first time, eliminates waste, and removes non-value-added costs at all stages." Through fundamental changes to Rockwell's structure, processes, and culture the company has realized dramatic improvements in productivity. They have gone from shipping 11 missiles per week to shipping 28 missiles per *day*, with one-third *fewer* employees. Their change effort has revived the company and turned Rockwell International back into a financial success story.[2]

ASEA BROWN BOVERI (ABB). This global electrical engineering giant is another example of a company that has made fundamental, large-scale changes in structure, process, and culture. ABB's CEO and president, Percy Barnevik, and his executive team dismantled the bureaucratic, hierarchical structure that is characteristic of many organizations and replaced it with 1,300 independently operated companies. What they created is an organization that is both big and small simultaneously. *Big* in the sense that the company uses its reputation to acquire large contracts and *small* in the sense that entrepreneurship is present within all 1,300 operating units.

But the change was not just structural. In a corporate culture based on mistrust, with limited decision-making at low levels of the organization, the heads of these 1,300 operating units would be little more than area supervisors ensuring that his or her unit, however far away from headquarters, was following orders from those at the top. According to Sumantra Ghosal and Christopher A. Bartlett, authors of *Managing Across Borders: The Transnational Solution*, ". . . traditional organizations usually break themselves into successively smaller entities to make it easier for top managers to allocate tasks and control performance." This is far from the case at ABB's operating units. Instead, the heads of these units run their business as if it were their own, with one exception—they share knowledge and information, via Business Area chief meetings, between all of the units.

Because these various units had access to the *best practices* from all operating units, this knowledge sharing made it possible for the company to successfully redesign the company's core processes in each Business Area. Furthermore, the information these individual units gain from their continuous learning and improvement of processes is transferred through the Business Area chiefs who are in frequent contact with the units in their own area.

Keys to a Successful Transformation

Companies that are creating and sustaining a competitive advantage are succeeding in areas where others have failed. Their success is due in a large part to the following actions:

- Going to extreme measures to involve employees in all aspects of the change effort
- Investing the time and resources necessary to formulate a strategic direction, and creating a clear change strategy that aligns all activities, systems, and processes to deliver superior value to customers
- Establishing a culture and system where all employees throughout the organization have the opportunity to learn, enabling them to continually improve their performance.

Each of these key success factors will be discussed in detail throughout the book. Because of the importance of getting employees involved in all aspects of the change effort, right from the beginning, the next section of this chapter examines ways in which management can ensure a high-level of employee involvement throughout the change process.

Getting Employees Involved

During a change effort, whether it be a companywide transformation or a small change initiative in a particular department, employees need to be highly involved. Employees perform at their best when management answers the following three questions:

1. "Why are we doing this?"
2. "How are we going to do this?"
3. "What is my role during and after?"

What employees are asking for is honest information about the change effort before they commit to it. Like anyone else, your employees want to know a few things before they say yes. To start, they want to know why they should take this journey and where it will take them. They might phrase this as, "Why are we doing this?" or "What will this new place look like?" Next, they want to know how they are going to get there: "Do we have a map?", "Who is going to drive?", or "Do we have a navigator?" might be some of the questions they are seeking answers to. Lastly, before they "get on board," they want to know if things are going to be any different where they are going, and if so, what will be different and what will remain the same.

Employees Must Know Why Change is Needed

The beginning of an organizational change effort is like the preparation for a long journey; the same concerns apply. You are asking your employees to commit to a change effort that will transform the way the organization does business. But in many cases the organization has been getting along pretty well for a long time, so many employees end up asking, "Why do we need to change?" The reasons for change may vary and even may be quite complicated, but management should in every instance freely and clearly communicate to employees the why.

Simply telling employees "the company is losing money" will not help them. They need specifics. If declining profits are the problem then you might point to the increasing competitiveness in the industry and the company's steadily decreasing market-share as the source of the problem. You might then explain how the decline in profitability has cut into the research and development and training budgets, and without new products in the pipeline and a well-trained workforce the company will be unable to compete effectively and will face financial instability in the upcoming years. Whatever the case for action, make sure the message is targeted to the appropriate audience.

Employees Need to Understand the Change Process

Once your employees understand why the company needs to undergo a change effort, you must explain to them how the company plans to get this done. Finding the balance of what each employee needs to know is important. Too much information will confuse most employees, while too little will leave many questions unanswered and fuel the rumor mill. The best approach is to give employees an overview of the change process—the scope, timeline, budget, consultants being used, and so on—and set aside plenty of time for a question and answer session.

When explaining the strategy and answering questions, communicate only the *facts*. If you know that one of the demands of the change effort is to reduce operating expenses by 20 percent, then tell your employees this. If you are unsure of how long this change effort will take but have a general idea, tell your employees you are unsure, but explain that similar change efforts at other companies have taken anywhere from 18 to 24 months.

Finally, employees want to know how the changes will affect them and what role they will play during and after the change process. Often they will ask, "What do I have to do?" and "When can I get back to my real work?" They need to understand that part of their real job is to promote and participate in the change effort. They need to understand that an organizational transformation will ultimately change their roles and responsibilities, creating new positions while eliminating some old ones. The underlying message to employees should be this: those who are committed to making the change effort a success and who are willing to be flexible and learn new skills have a place in the future organization.

Tap into the Potential of the Entire Workforce
Though it is crucial for frontline employees to participate in the change effort, it is equally, if not more important to define the role these employees will play in the future organization. The newly transformed organization must tap into the potential of the entire workforce if its goal is to add significant value to the customer. A change effort that cuts costs, reduces headcount, and attracts new business, while failing to tap into and link together the knowledge and energy of everyone in the

organization, will not be truly successful. If a change effort leaves individuals in positions that block others from learning, or leaves systems in place that keep information from those who need it, the company is not realizing the true potential of its workforce and will lose out to those competitors that do.

The Need for Speed and Innovation

Even in the fiercely competitive global business environment of the late 1990s, many organizations are still based on the traditional mass-producing business model developed in the first half and middle of the 20th century. This traditional model is rooted in the belief that a top-down, control-oriented bureaucratic management structure, with workers performing repetitive, specialized jobs requiring no thought, is the most efficient way to organize and run a company. This model was effective from 1945 to the early 1970s because the competitive environment was stable, the workforce was primarily uneducated, and consumers in the United States and the developed world demanded manufactured goods (almost regardless of the level of quality) in unprecedented quantities.

In the early 1970s, several changes occurred simultaneously in the business arena that brought into question the efficiency and effectiveness of this traditional model. International competition was increasing as the Japanese and Germans completed their post-war industrial rebuilding. Additionally, U.S. workers were becoming better educated and were demanding better working conditions. Finally, the international demand for U.S.-made products began to drop, and foreign-made products, which were cheaper and offered comparable or even higher quality, were being imported into the United States in ever-increasing numbers.

Today's business environment is even more competitive. The pressure is no longer just from Japan and Germany, but from Korea, Taiwan, India, Singapore, Thailand, and many other nations. Even though these countries have the ability to pay workers lower wages, they are not competing solely on the basis of price itself. Instead, many of them are becoming strong competitors because they have a highly educated workforce, high rate of national savings, and productive corporations.

Simply cutting costs and producing higher-quality goods and services will not be enough to remain competitive in this decade and beyond. First-class quality and low prices (which determine value) are no longer the key elements needed to succeed in any industry, they are the *standards* for doing business. Speed and innovation are now replacing quality and price as the sole determinants of success. According to Noel Tichy and Stratford Sherman, authors of *Control Your Destiny or Someone Else Will*, "Once all surviving contenders in a market can offer value, the battle shifts to speed and innovation. To distinguish themselves, companies must offer something unique. They are all racing to find the new ideas, the new processes, that will position them to win customers."[3]

In a bureaucratic organization where no clear strategic direction is in place, where rules and procedures are written to cover every possible situation, and where employees are commanded and controlled because the culture is based on mistrust, it is impossible to be quick and innovative, or to create, let alone sustain, a competitive advantage. A company that cannot respond quickly to its customers, foster new ideas for products, services, and processes, or trust its employees is a company doomed to failure.

Companies lacking a clear strategic direction, that have unaligned processes, or have yet to tap into the potential of their entire workforce or make learning available to all employees, must consider an organizational transformation. Small, incremental change programs in these areas will fall short of making the necessary improvements to create a competitive advantage, both domestically and abroad. By taking the bolder step of launching a well-planned and coordinated transformation effort, you can reconstruct your whole organization, an organization that can provide the highest value to your customers while giving you the best opportunity to succeed in today's competitive marketplace.

When an organizational transformation is successful, the advantages will be many. Customer service and satisfaction will dramatically increase. The new flexibility will enable the organization to respond to competitors and customers in time to avoid potentially devastating losses to market share, revenues, etc. Additionally, the organization will experience increased employee motivation, higher quality goods and services, and dramatic cost-savings. Together, these advantages mean long-term success for an organization's customers, employees, managers, and shareholders.

In Chapter 2, we will discuss the role of the CEO or Executive Team. The focus will be on the type of leader (change agent) needed to *champion* an organizational transformation and the specific elements he or she must establish before beginning this revolution in the workplace.

Establish Transformational Leadership

"What is required is . . . a new philosophy of leadership that is always and at all times focused on enlisting the hearts and minds of followers through inclusion and participation. Such a philosophy must be rooted in the most fundamental of moral principles: respect for people."

— James O'Toole[1]
(AUTHOR OF *Leading Change*)

Organizations attempting a transformation need transformational leaders throughout the company. What characteristics do transformational leaders possess? What must these leaders do in order to prepare their organizations for all of the difficult challenges that lie ahead?

Transformational Leaders vs. Traditional Leaders

According to Bernard M. Bass, the director of the Center for Leadership Studies at the State University of New York at Binghamton, *transactional* (or *traditional*) leaders get things done by promising and rewarding good performers, while threatening and disciplining poor performers. Today, a new type of leader must emerge. Traditional leaders must be replaced by *transformational* leaders if an organization is going to

17

successfully change. A transformational leader is characterized as one who inspires followers with his or her vision, gains respect and trust, and intellectually challenges employees.[2] What really separates a transformational leader from a transactional leader is that the latter is distant and impersonal, while the transformational leader is intensely interpersonal. This closeness allows the transformational leader to give employees personal attention and to identify with them, an important first step in establishing a relationship built on trust.

While transactional leaders at best maintain the status quo, transformational leaders generate the total organizational support needed to carry out the changes described in this book. And without employee support, a change effort has no realistic chance of ever being implemented. In fact, ". . . employees say that they themselves exert extra effort on behalf of managers who are transformational leaders."[3]

But transformational leadership characteristics alone do not ensure a successful corporate transformation. There are several crucial elements the transformation leader must establish *before* any organizational transformation can even get started. Although these elements will be discussed separately, it is important to understand that when taken together they form a launching platform for leaders to begin the organizational transformation process. The responsibilities of transformational leaders prior to beginning a transformation include:

- Developing and communicating a clear strategic direction
- Building top management support for the change effort
- Establishing and demonstrating new cultural values

Developing a Clear Strategic Direction

Unlike efforts that seek to empower employees, redesign a process, revise a compensation system, or create a team-based organization, a transformation effort must be rooted in a strategy that calls for drastic, large-scale change. More than anything else, it is the leader's job to formulate and communicate this new strategic direction.

Formulating the Strategic Direction

With the recent focus on process improvement and cost cutting, one might think that organizational success is the sole result of operating the most efficiently within an industry. Certainly, organizations benefit from making improvements in systems and processes, but real success demands a much different kind of investment. Truly successful organizations create and sustain a lasting competitive advantage by formulating a unique strategy that:

- Links together all companywide activities into a value-adding delivery chain
- Taps into the potential of all employees
- Establishes a continuous learning and improvement culture

To formulate a unique strategy that adds value to a desired segment of the market, you must examine the existing competencies of the organization, the current market conditions, who your customer is, and the competition. In addition, you must factor in educated predictions about the future needs of customers and the developments and uses of new technology. With the current emphasis on delivering ever greater value to customers, it will be helpful to discuss what is meant by the

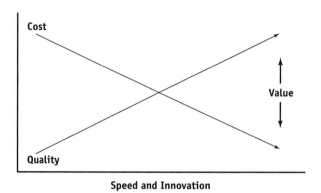

Figure 2-1. A Value Graph

term *value*. A useful way to think of value is illustrated above in Figure 2-1.

This simple diagram shows that value is determined by the customer's perception of the difference between product or service quality and price and the degree of speed and innovation. In the past, it was thought that one could increase product quality, lower cost, or increase speed, but not all three. This trade-off mentality has changed.

Today, the challenge to deliver value lies not only in increasing quality and lowering cost, but also in making hard choices regarding what customers are demanding and how best to serve that demand. Once companies choose their strategic direction—deciding what their customers want and what markets to compete in—their challenge switches to aligning the systems, structure, and culture to make the strategic goals a reality.

As Michael Porter wrote in his *Harvard Business Review* article, ". . . strategy involves a whole system of activities, not a collection of parts. Competitive advantage comes from the way these activities fit and reinforce one another."[4] This is precisely the reason why organizations pursuing a new strategic direction and undergoing a transformation must reconstruct the whole company—the structure, systems, and culture. By improving, changing, and aligning each of these components you create a new level of fit among activities that in turn will create and sustain a competitive advantage.

Communicating the Strategic Direction

Prior to initiating any type of large-scale change effort, employees need to understand the company's strategy so they can make decisions consistent with the company's goals. Without a clearly communicated strategic direction the change effort will lack the focus needed to mobilize employees to commit to doing what is necessary to realize the company's vision. Leaders must go to great lengths to educate their employees about the company's strategic direction. Simply announcing the new strategy or distributing it via e-mail or video is not enough. If leaders expect employees to be able to refer to the strategy during day-to-day decision making, then employees must truly understand it. This requires significant employee education by face-to-face meetings between employees and their managers or team leaders.

Because most organizations refer to financial models, statements, or graphs in devising their strategies, it is crucial that the company educate the employees on the financial aspects of the business. As employees become more empowered and responsible for the success of the organization, they must understand how the company makes, manages, and allocates money. In his book *Open-Book Management*, John Case writes about the importance of educating everyone on the company's financials. Compared to a conventional businesses, employees in open-book companies ". . . know whether they are making money. They know how much. They know why. They have a pretty good idea of what the future holds—all because they see the numbers that most companies show only to top managers."[5]

In newly transformed organizations, employees not only see the numbers, they move the numbers in the right direction. But how do they know that what they do every day is helping to improve the company's bottom line? This is where management must be responsible for making and displaying a direct link between the activities of each employee, the performance of their area of responsibility, and the performance of the entire company. Whether it is a salesperson in the company's Northeast region, an assembly line worker in an automotive plant, or a customer service representative for an airline, to get the most out of each employee that employee must feel that the work they do is valuable to the company. One of the best ways to show an employee that their work is valuable is to let them see the impact their performance has on a larger piece of the business.

For example, imagine that you are a manager of a fast-food franchise and some of your employees are having problems seeing how their performance impacts the rest of the company; this in turn is affecting their attitude and quality of work. As the manager you need to motivate your employees at all times to perform at their best. You know that if your employees understand the link between their performance and the performance of the store and overall company, they will take greater pride in and feel more responsible about their jobs. How do you explain this to a particular employee?

You start by showing how their performance is impacting the rest of the crew members. Next, you establish a connection between the performance of their crew and the performance of other crews. Then you show how the results of each of these crews directly impact the profitability of the franchise and in turn the entire company.

Take soft drinks for example. Because soft drinks are highly profitable, every time an employee suggests a larger drink size to a customer and that customer accepts, he or she is increasing the profitability of his shift. If every shift worker focuses on selling more soft drinks the whole store will be more profitable. By making the connection between individual sales performance and store profitability you can then make a link between the profitability of this franchise, the profitability of the region, and the overall financial results of the organization.

The fast-food restaurant scorecard illustrated in Figure 2-2 makes a financial link between the activities of employee teams and the performance of the store, region, and whole organization. By focusing individuals and teams at every level on a balanced set of activities, e.g., customer satisfaction, selling, etc., every employee can positively impact the overall performance of the organization.

As will be discussed in Chapter 10, to strengthen the link between employee and company performance, management should provide a financial link between the performance of employees, their teams, and the company or business unit. When this link is in place, your employees can see how their performance impacts the organization's bottom line. This kind of linkage also goes a long way in increasing employees' motivation to improve.

Building Top Management Support

The next major responsibility of leadership is to build top management support for the change effort. For any full-scale organizational change effort to succeed, top management must not

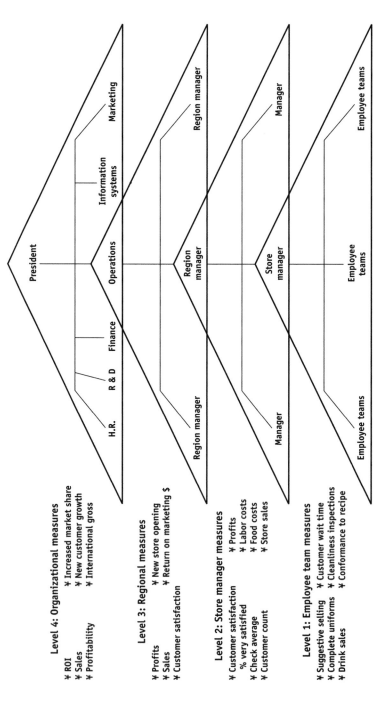

Level 4: Organizational measures

* ROI   * Increased market share
* Sales   * New customer growth
* Profitability   * International gross

Level 3: Regional measures

* Profits   * New store opening
* Sales   * Return on marketing $
* Customer satisfaction

Level 2: Store manager measures

* Customer satisfaction   * Profits
  % very satisfied   * Labor costs
* Check average   * Food costs
* Customer count   * Store sales

Level 1: Employee team measures

* Suggestive selling   * Customer wait time
* Complete uniforms   * Cleanliness inspections
* Drink sales   * Conformance to recipe

Figure 2-2. A Fast-Food Restaurant Scorecard

only support the changes but also be the driving force behind the planning and development of the changes. However, top management's contribution certainly does not stop here. The most important responsibility of the CEO or senior management team is to lead the organization into and through the implementation phase. If the leadership team's commitment to the change effort diminishes while the design is still on paper, the design will remain on paper, with little chance of it ever being implemented.

Small-scale, incremental improvements in operations or procedures or minor changes in organizational structure can be led by middle-level managers and teams. But in an organizational transformation, nothing short of complete senior management leadership and support will suffice. This is not to say that all but senior-level employees are left out of this change process. Rather, the CEO and his or her senior management team is responsible for soliciting and incorporating the ideas, suggestions, and comments, positive or negative, from individuals throughout the organization. They should acquire information from outside the company as well—from customers, potential customers, suppliers, competitors, stockholders, and other crucial groups.

At the center of the CEO's job is the need to create an integrated, balanced, well-thought-out transformation plan unique to the company, one that the top management team can support. Simply providing an ad hoc jumble of programs and policy changes will not be enough to convince senior managers that this is a change plan that moves the company toward its vision.

In my interview with David Baldwin, a Malcolm Baldrige Quality Examiner and Independent Business Consultant, he discussed the importance of creating a detailed and well-integrated change plan:[6]

> Too many organizations fail because they don't do appropriate planning. Instead of developing a complete and detailed change plan that targets the areas of the organization that need particular improvement or drastic redesign, these companies let their employees decide what improvements to work on. The employees with this new responsibility, in most cases, are not provided with adequate training and frequently lack access to the information necessary for appropriate decision-making to take place. It is these same executives who then say that Reengineering or TQM doesn't work.

Declaring top management's complete support for this dramatic change will help employees understand that the organization as a whole is completely behind this transformation process. Anything short of this will suggest to employees that changes will be required of only those outside the domain of senior management, or that top management does not truly believe that the organization needs to transform in order to succeed in the marketplace.

But senior managers need to do more than just declare their support for the change effort, they must demonstrate an ongoing commitment every day. Successfully transforming an organization through a large-scale change effort does not happen overnight. The company constantly must be focused and committed to the change effort throughout the long haul. There is only one way to pull this off: the daily commitment to the change process by all types of leaders. This will motivate others to stick to it and keep the change effort alive and moving forward.

One way for top managers to show their support for the changes that are underway is to always make time to answer questions raised by their associates. When senior managers take a moment to respond to a simple question, or spend an hour with a small group of employees confused about a particular aspect of the transformation, they are communicating more to their employees than just the answers to their questions. They are sending the message that the change effort is so important to the future of the organization that they are personally making every effort possible to ensure its success.

Senior managers can also show their commitment by providing employees with access to training, information, and external support that is not normally within their reach. A senior manager that restructures the budget so that employees can acquire the resources needed to make the change effort a success sends a powerful signal that top management believes and supports the employee efforts.

Establishing New Cultural Values

The final responsibility of leadership before beginning an organizational transformation is to develop a new set of cultural values. For most organizations in need of dramatic organizational change, the company culture is often militaristic, based on mistrust, and adverse to risk. These are all characteristics that are the opposite of General Electric's culture, which is based on the premise that "Workers who share their employer's goals (and values) don't need much supervision."[7]

BELLSOUTH. This company struggled with many of the cultural issues that surface during an organizational transformation. Like other large companies, BellSouth had an institutional mentality that made change extremely difficult. Therefore, getting employees to change their attitudes and behaviors was a significant challenge. "Changing corporate culture is one of the most demanding challenges any company faces because it takes time and requires far more than edict from on high," says Becky Dunn, BellSouth Vice President/Human Resources and Benefits Administration.[8] Another voice from inside the company stresses the importance of changing the corporate culture. "The key to making the cultural transition successful," says Dale Register, BellSouth Assistant Vice President/Reengineering, "is to have the employees help spread the *new corporate ideology*, because relying on management to communicate the new philosophy will not be enough."[9]

If the key to making cultural change successful is getting employees to help spread the new corporate ideology, as Dale Register of BellSouth says, then the challenge is to get employees to talk positively about the new philosophy. But how do you do that? The only way employees will become excited and talk about something new, especially a new corporate ideology, is if they themselves believe in it. The best way you can help employees see the value in creating a new company culture is by providing them with role models who will demonstrate the new cultural values. In other words, in creating a new company culture, the leaders of the organization must take these three steps:

1. Demonstrate a firm commitment to this new culture
2. Endorse the changes taking place
3. Act as true spokespeople (role models)

Having laid out the new corporate ideology, how do you establish a new set of cultural values? What is this new culture I am talking about? It is a culture where there is a foundation of:

- Mutual trust throughout the organization
- Two-way communication of open, honest information
- Continuous learning and growth for all employees

Without this foundation a change effort will struggle to get off the ground and experience difficulty sustaining any momentum. And the company will never actually arrive at the planned destination. A company where employees don't trust their leaders or coworkers, don't share information, and don't have an opportunity to learn is a company that will never realize any long-term benefits of even the best transformation plan.

Mutual Trust Throughout the Organization

The most important cultural issue leaders should be aware of is establishing an atmosphere of *mutual trust* throughout the organization. "As the level of trust increases," says John H. Zenger, President of Zenger-Miller, Inc., "employees are able to achieve more of their potential as individuals and to make greatly expanded contributions to the organization."[10] Initially, employees will resist "buying-into" management's call for change. They will suspect that their jobs are at stake, that they are going to be told to work harder, and that the talk of change is only temporary and will be over by the end of the month or fiscal quarter. According to Hagood Bellinger, Executive-in-Residence at Georgia Institute of Technology's Graduate School of Management, "Even if the message gets repeated enough and employees understand that change is inevitable, employees will do everything they can to make sure the changes do not work, because they are sure that the new system or structure will be used to gain greater control over their work or to eliminate their jobs."[11]

In many cases employees need not worry about having to work in a truly redesigned or transformed setting. The reason?

When a company's culture is rooted in mistrust and suspicion of others, and this does not change, management will fail to remove the checks and controls, e.g., authorization signatures, duplicated work efforts, etc., that are eliminated during a true transformation effort. An organization determined to create a culture based on trust and mutual respect must establish the following basic principles.

- *Total Involvement.* Everyone in the organization must participate in order to change the culture. An organization's culture is the sum of its members' habits. This includes how decisions are made, how people dress, how people communicate, how conflict is resolved, and so on. You cannot change a culture without everyone in the organization participating in the change.
- *Diversity.* Differences in thought and opinion add value to the end product. Compliance and conformance are not necessarily good things, but individuals often try to fit in to avoid causing any conflict. This assimilation process often denies teams exposure to other ways of doing things. If you want everyone on all teams to maximize their creativity, solve their complex problems, and have total involvement in the company, they will need to explore and accept the intellectual, emotional, and cultural differences between them.
- *Listening.* Listening to others shows them the greatest form of respect. Listening is the most fundamental step in showing others how much you value their suggestions or ideas. An organizational culture that doesn't stress the importance of active listening will not foster trust and mutual respect for others and their ideas.
- *Recognition.* People perform at higher levels of excellence when given appropriate recognition. Everyone needs recogni-

ESTABLISH TRANSFORMATIONAL LEADERSHIP   31

tion. Whether a CEO, file clerk, scientist, or factory worker, at the end of the day we want to go home feeling "that was a job well done." Every member of the organization has the responsibility of providing recognition to others.

Another way to establish trust in your organization is to never "beat around the bush" when communicating with your employees. By being direct with people you will promote trust as a shared value and establish yourself as someone your employees can believe in. People don't like sugarcoated messages, so don't give them to your employees. If you are presenting fourth-quarter earnings that are well below expectations, don't waste people's time by trying to hide it. Instead, come straight out and communicate the facts. Then, spend the majority of your time talking about what the company will do differently to increase earnings next quarter, and be prepared to answer tough questions.

Just as important as being direct with people is giving honest responses, even responses that you know your listeners will dislike. You will diminish any trust that you have established within your organization if you mislead your employees or withhold the truth for fear that your employees won't want to hear the bad news. Employees want the facts, even if they mean job reductions or budget cutbacks—then at least they will be in a position to make informed decisions concerning their future. In the absence of facts, employees speculate, stress-out, and rely on the rumor mill as their information source; then they use this rumor-based information when making decisions about the company and their future.

Encouraging your employees to challenge leaders without fear of reprisals is another very important element in building trust. Unfortunately, in most companies employees do not feel confident and safe enough to stand up and challenge their bosses without fear of reprisal. It is the leader's responsibility to create a culture where employees can challenge ideas and decisions—as long as it is conducted in an assertive and constructive manner. This means that top management must go beyond just dictating to the managers to provide their employees with an open forum to challenge and debate ideas and decisions they strongly oppose. Instead, like all of these new cultural values, the leader's actions must be visible—this is the only way to convince employees that things have really changed in the company. Only then will they truly feel it is safe to stand up and be heard.

Words, either contained in speeches, videos, or visual statements, have very little effect compared with face-to-face interaction. Trust is built when employees observe nonthreatening and honest behavior on the part of their manager. If, for example, during a meeting employees see their manager listening to someone challenging his or her idea, without being berated either in public or behind closed doors, trust begins to take root. When this type of interaction occurs repeatedly, trust is established and will remain in place, unless the manager does something to jeopardize the trust he or she has worked so hard to create.

Two-Way Communication Flow of Open and Honest Information

To continue building mutual trust and to develop a new corporate culture, the organization must create a two-way communication flow of open and honest information between managers and employees—an open communication that permeates the entire organization. A two-way communication flow means that managers and subordinates alike both express their opinions and actively listen to one another. According to Jack Welch, CEO of General Electric, "Direct, personal, two-way communication is what seems to make the difference. Exposing people—without the protection of title or position—to ideas from everywhere. Judging ideas on their merits."[12] This type of communication flow enables (and requires) everyone in the organization to make contributions, without regard to rank or title. This is especially important for a successful organizational transformation because it takes everyone's involvement and contribution to make the change process work.

A two-way communication flow helps to break down what in many companies is the cultural norm—that only the people at the top of the organization have the right ideas and solutions to solve all of the company's problems. Without a system for idea exchange, the level of employee contributions will vary widely within an organization, depending on the type of manager/ leader in each division or unit.

Organizations should establish communication guidelines, but remember that descriptions of new values found in newsletters, memos, speeches, or videos, mean nothing when actions don't support what has been stated. The following list provides communication values that leaders need to demonstrate if employees are to believe cultural changes are taking place.

- Ideas are based on their merit, not on the contributor
- Everyone has an opportunity to share their knowledge, information, and/or opinion
- Forms of communication should be varied and take advantage of the advances in information technology
- Constructive and assertive behavior is required
- Everyone is expected to actively listen before responding or passing judgment

Continuous Learning and Growth for All Employees

A third value needed to create a new culture capable of getting the most out of each employee is *continuous learning for all*. The absence of continuous learning means that employees cannot contribute to the knowledge base of the company. Therefore the company will have to rely solely on outsiders or senior managers to inject new knowledge into the organization. In cultivating a new corporate culture, leaders must understand the importance of rooting the culture in the belief that continuous learning applies to and is available to all individuals in the corporation. Simply put, for an organization to continually improve, everyone must continuously learn. It is the leader's role to build this type of *learning organization*.

According to Peter M. Senge, Director of the Systems Thinking and Organizational Learning program at the MIT Sloan School of Management, "Leaders in learning organizations are responsible for *building organizations* where people are continually expanding their capabilities to shape their future — that is, leaders are responsible for learning."[13] Leaders start building learning organizations by focusing their time and the organization's attention on the underlying causes of the problems that exist in the company. Effective leaders then challenge their workers to develop solutions that will permanently fix the problem. This type of learning environment increases the likelihood for organizational success by enhancing the capabilities of the entire workforce.

Without continual learning for all, you cannot expect your employees to embrace an organizational change effort. For your employees to be key players in the successful change effort, a leader needs to set aside time and money to inform them about the details of the change strategy, educate them about why the change is required, and teach them new skills so they can be part of the company's future.

Relying on just a few top managers to gather all of the information, make all of the decisions, and orchestrate the transformation of all human and physical resources only increases the knowledge of a few, while the other 99% of the organization learns more about following orders. Not only does this severely jeopardize the change effort, but the potential learning experience through teaching employees about benchmarking, improving customer service, redesigning processes, and measuring performance is lost forever. More detailed information concerning the importance of organizational learning will be provided in Chapter 11.

Chapter 3 explains how leaders can lead effective change by creating an environment that fosters participation and ownership. It also presents a change management plan that details the activities and actions necessary to manage a successful organizational transformation.

Guide Effective and Lasting Change

"Most of the time we try to convince people that change is going to be better. Instead we should try to pull them into the visioning process."

— KARIN KOLODOZIEJSKI
(HUMAN RESOURCES MANAGER, TEKTRONIX)

Providing employees with the means to participate in and take ownership of the change effort is central in leading effective and lasting change. In addition, organizational leaders must make sure employees understand the current state of the organization by defining the current reality, why it must transform, what it is transforming into, and how it will make the transformation. Leaders must also create an environment that fosters participation and ownership. Said another way, leaders can learn to "practice the art of inclusion."[1] Along with discussing these issues, this chapter will also present a change management plan detailing the activities and actions necessary to manage a successful organizational transformation.

Fostering Employee Participation and Ownership

Whether trying to change an individual's behavior or the structure, systems, and culture of an organization, those most successful at leading change begin by listening to those who are being asked to change. Only by listening to the needs, wants, and concerns of those involved in a change effort can leaders begin to formulate a change direction that considers everyone in the organization.

Those senior managers that fail to listen, especially at the beginning of a large-scale change effort, quickly send the message that the needs, wants, and concerns of anyone or everyone in the organization come second to what senior management deems to be important. As a result, this authoritarian style of management fails to generate any of the needed organizational support for the change effort.

This lack of organizational support, or more generally speaking, this resistance to change, is to be expected anytime individuals are commanded to do something, even if it's in their best interest. James O'Toole, in his book *Leading Change: Overcoming the Ideology of Comfort and the Tyranny of Custom*, acknowledges this when he explains why individuals refuse to become followers. "The major source of resistance to change," says O'Toole, "is the all-too-human objection to having the will of others imposed on us."[2]

If it can be agreed upon that no one wants the will of others imposed on them, then how can leaders encourage followers to make those changes that are in their own, and their company's, best interest? The answer lies in not only soliciting ideas and insights from employees throughout the organization, but in engaging employees in *every* aspect of the transformation effort—in effect, giving the employees ownership of the changes. It is only after totally involving the employees can the whole organization increase the pace of the change effort and concentrate fully on creating a lasting competitive advantage.

Change Management Plan

The change management plan is built on the foundation established in the beginning of this chapter: *for any change effort to be successful, employees must not only have a strong voice in setting the direction for the changes, but be active participants and owners of every stage of the change process.* The term owners or ownership is not meant to imply that senior management lacks formal authority for the change effort, but, rather, that employees and management jointly share responsibility for transforming the organization. The following change management plan contains seven stages:

1. Undergo an industry and organizational assessment
2. Create and communicate a positive vision of the future
3. Establish and communicate a case for action and sense of urgency
4. Define and communicate the new strategic direction and specific organizational performance goals
5. Establish and communicate the change strategy as the link between current performance and desired future performance goals
6. Seek out and celebrate easily attainable, but important, early successes and reinforce behavior consistent with company values
7. Make change and continual improvement a way of life for the organization

Stage 1: Undergo an Organization and Industry Assessment

What type of culture exists in the organization? How are employees treated? Do employees have input? What is the nature of the organization's business? What are the critical success factors for this industry? What segment(s) are we competing in? What products and/or services are we delivering? What is our relationship with customers? With suppliers? With partners?

Leaders must first have a handle on where their organization currently stands before beginning any transformation process. Once again I refer to the remarks of David Baldwin, a Malcolm Baldrige Quality Examiner: "The best way to assess the current state of your organization is to listen to the Four Voices—those of the Customer, Employee, Process, and Stockholder."[3] In addition, leaders should undertake a comprehensive industry assessment in order to develop a strategic direction for the organization, a direction that builds or enhances core competencies that result in a lasting competitive advantage.

Voice of the Customer

Listening to the customer about product or service quality, delivery time, and degree of satisfaction, among other measures and perceptions, informs management and employees on how the organization is performing in the areas crucial to its success. Without the customer's input, senior managers typically make the mistake of basing their decisions on their perceptions of the business environment, instead of on what the business environment is actually telling them.

Voice of the Employee

For the same reasons management listens to the voice of the customer, they should listen to their employees. J. Richard

Hackman, Professor of Social and Organizational Psychology at Harvard University, proposes using a simple four-question checklist to assess the role employees play in the organization:

1. Who decides?
2. Who is responsible?
3. Who learns?
4. Who gains?[4]

Finding the answers to these questions will determine whether the organization taps into the potential of all employees.

Voice of the Process

By listening to the voice of the process, meaning on-time delivery, system error percentages, and so on, and benchmarking these processes against competitors and world-class performers—senior management and employees together can determine how dramatic the process redesign needs to be. This voice will also help with decisions about how critical the time frame is for process redesign.

Voice of the Stockholder

The stockholder provides the organization's leaders with the important overall indicators of the firm's performance. Measurements such as return on investment (ROI), revenue growth, and sales per employee, can easily be used to benchmark the competition. Too often these financial measurements or stockholder voices are the only thing management listens to. However, with attention to the first three voices, the leaders will know what changes to make and how to go about making them.

Listening only to the stockholder is a mistake because the numbers they provide represent past performance, providing no information regarding likely future performance. Companies that have traditionally relied on the voices of the stockholder often find it difficult to convince their employees that change is needed for the long-term success of the company. In these companies, employees have been trained to focus on improving the stock price, so they easily dismiss management proclamations concerning change, especially when short-term figures indicate rising annual earnings and an increasing stock value. To counter this, leaders need to educate management and employees on the importance of using all four voices to assess current and likely future performance. This will help convince employees why and when change is needed, and the data from these four assessments will provide them with the proactive information they need to change their piece of the business.

Transforming an organization with only present business conditions and current organizational considerations in mind might create a new organization capable of short-term success, but will certainly fail to position the organization for longer-term market dominance or excellence. To avoid this mistake and position the organization for long-term success, organizational leaders and employees must continually seek to create and take advantage of future opportunities that are constantly occurring in the marketplace.

Gary Hamel and C. K. Prahalad, in their book *Competing for the Future: Breakthrough Strategies for Seizing Control of Your Industry and Creating the Markets of Tomorrow*, examine in detail the need for organizations to not only transform themselves, but also to transform the industries they compete in:

> Competition for the future is competition to create and dominate emerging opportunities—to stake out new com-

petitive space. Creating the future is more challenging than playing catch up, in that you have to create your own road map. The goal is not simply to benchmark a competitor's products and processes and imitate its methods, but to develop an independent point of view about tomorrow's opportunities and how to exploit them.[5]

Just as important as gathering accurate and relevant information during these assessments is the need to have all employees believe that the information is a realistic portrayal of the organization and industry conditions. Instead of trying to force employees to digest large quantities of industry and organizational assessment data that was gathered by a select group of top managers, organizations should provide a means for as many employees as possible to participate in the external benchmarking and internal assessment process.

While it is acknowledged that not everyone in a large organization can attend site visits and focus groups, creative communication by joint employee and management report-out teams can spread the findings of these benchmarking and data-gathering trips. Communication devices, such as discussion lunches, conferences, internal newsletters, meetings, and selected readings, are terrific information-sharing mechanisms, particularly when the information is seen as coming from other employees—not just from top management.

Stage 2: Create and Communicate a Positive Vision of the Future

It is up to the leaders of organizations to rally their employees around the change effort. But before any leader attempts to establish the change imperative—convincing the employees *why* the entire company must change — he or she must first paint a picture of what the company is striving to become. Leaders can use this opportunity to inspire employees by giving them a glimpse at the vision of the *future state of the organization*.

Few other vision statements are as profound as the Rev. Martin Luther King's "I Have A Dream" speech. It was through his vision that his followers, and all Americans, imagined a future that they did not think was possible. It is this type of imagination that creates the sense in individuals that a new type of future is possible if they put their collective energies together to make it happen.

SOUTHLAND LIFE. The visioning process (vision-creation process) is often the collective work of various members of an organization. At Southland Life, an Atlanta-based insurance company, the CEO inspired the employees with the picture of the future state of the organization. To develop the vision, he formed a "Vision Team," made up of a cross section of employees throughout the organization, to come up with the words for the company's new vision.[6] This *co-development*, where management and staff work hand-in-hand in planning and developing the future organization, is one of the key elements that make organizational change successful.

U.S. CONTINENTAL DIVISION OF ROYAL/DUTCH SHELL. There are many forms of co-development in creating the future vision of an organization. The U.S. Continental Division of Royal/ Dutch Shell invited over 100 employees from throughout the organization to participate in a two-day Direction Setting Workshop. At this workshop, participants reflected on their past experiences with the company, discussed trends affecting their company and industry, and spent a considerable amount

of time visualizing how to design the new organization to cap-
italize on these trends. The participants even went so far as to
form into teams and present creative skits that helped their fellow participants visualize what the future of the organization
could be.

FORD MOTOR COMPANY. Donald Peterson, CEO of Ford Motor
Company, understands the importance of basing a strong and
clearly communicated vision and value statement on the needs
of the people who make up Ford's marketplace. For example,
when he became CEO of the company, quality was a major
concern of Ford customers. From listening to his employees
and the *voices of the processes*, he understood that the company
was far from their quality goals—resulting in the well-known
company *value* "Quality is Job 1." This value statement is not
only appropriate because it reflects the voice of the customers
—it is also clear and concise. Ford employees not only can easily understand the company value, they can incorporate it into
decisions made during their everyday work.

Experts agree on the importance of establishing a vision.
According to Larry Miller, President of the Miller Howard
Consulting Group, Inc:

> Change begins with a belief, a philosophy with values. To be
> achieved, a vision of what your organization should be is re-
> quired. It is visions of the future, our destiny, our mission,
> and our purpose that energize people. Ambition, drive, and
> sacrifice are all related to the strength of vision held by a
> group of people.[7]

Along with being far-reaching and energizing people, a
company's vision and value statement must be relevant in the
marketplace. "For organizations," says James A. Belasco, the

chairman of Management Development Associates and author of *Teaching Elephants to Dance*, "the vision should be based on the needs of the people who make up its marketplace."[8]

Most importantly, for the vision and values to be effective, leaders must act in accordance with the vision and values statement. A failure on the part of leaders to use the vision and values as a set of guiding principles will undoubtedly lead to employees thinking that the vision/value statement is really nothing more than fancy words framed and put on the wall. Leaders can take immediate steps to support their new vision and values by acting in accordance with the new principles from day one.

Stage 3: Establish and Communicate a Case for Action and Sense of Urgency

A clearly stated and carefully crafted positive vision for the future will fail to inspire or motivate employees to change unless they understand *why* change is needed. That is why information such as an increasing number of customer complaints, the loss of market share, the loss of new business, and so on must be made available to employees and communicated in a personal way such that everyone in the organization feels threatened by their company's poor performance. The more visible the crisis, the more willing employees will be to change; they will see the change effort as being less scary than doing nothing.

Having employees involved in the gathering of information through assessments and benchmarking, as discussed previously, goes a long way in helping to convince them that change is needed. Regardless of the role employees play in gathering company or industry data, everyone throughout the organization must understand what this information means to the health and financial performance of the organization. "Employees and managers at all levels must believe the data," says Edgar H. Schein in his working paper entitled *How Can Organizations Learn Faster? The Problem of Entering the Green Room*,[9] "and that often requires *intense communication and economic education*, something that has often been missing in organizations, so employees simply do not understand or do not believe it when management says 'we are in trouble.'"

But leaders must do more than just provide the case for action for the organization. They need to communicate the negative information in a personal, more meaningful way. Schein goes on to say in his working paper that even if employees believe the data to be a realistic portrayal of business and industry conditions, it may not motivate them to change because they do not connect the information to something they care about. The motivation to change occurs only when individuals feel anxious about failing to meet some of their important goals, or when their jobs or security are in jeopardy. "We have all seen," says Schein, "how employees do not take management information seriously until they feel personally threatened or feel ashamed or guilty because they are not living up to their own ideals or aspirations."

Fostering feelings of anxiety or guilt in employees can only go so far in ensuring that changes will begin taking place. If an environment of *psychological safety* is not set up, these high levels of anxiety and stress can actually prevent employees from making changes. Schein concludes his working paper by stating:

> For change to happen, for motivation to arise to learn something new, people have to feel psychologically safe, by which I mean that they will see a path forward that is manageable,

a direction of change that will not be catastrophic, in the sense that the person changing will still feel a sense of identity and wholeness. In organizational life powerful visions articulated by charismatic leaders can sometimes provide the necessary psychological safety, provided they not only sketch out a desired longer-range sense of direction, but also some immediate steps that are manageable and psychologically safe.[10]

Some of the elements that go into creating a psychologically safe environment include:

- Providing employees with opportunities for training and practice
- Providing support and encouragement to help employees begin working in this new environment
- Providing employees with a clear sense of the direction the company is heading by clearly communicating a change road map

Stage 4: Define and Communicate the New Strategic Direction and Specific Organizational Performance Goals

Organizational transformations are undertaken to generate dramatic improvements in business performance and customer satisfaction. By defining and communicating the new strategic direction and specific organizational improvement goals, leaders of a transformation can help employees focus their efforts and energy on the key areas of the business that will determine future success.

A change program with too many initiatives confuses participants and inevitably drains energy and resources away from the handful of goals that supersede all others. By focusing the organization on a few specific stretch goals, employees can then track progress and evaluate whether each activity they perform helps the company move closer to its overall goals.

When Rockwell International's Tactical Systems Division went about its transformation, the company set clear performance improvement goals that everyone in the organization understood. Despite the intense competition in the rapidly declining defense industry, the company could excel by 1) doing things right the first time, 2) eliminating waste, and 3) removing non-value-added costs at all stages.

When the organization specifies clear performance improvement goals, employees must align their activities and measures with the overall goals of the company. Only when employees clearly understand the key business objectives can they brainstorm ways in which they can impact these important areas. If, for example, employees and managers understand that one of their company's key business objectives is to grow market share, they can increase the time spent on new product development or budget more resources for advertising and promotion. Without this knowledge, these employees and managers would be operating in the dark about how to prioritize activities and allocate resources.

Stage 5: Establish and Communicate the Change Strategy as the Link Between Current Performance and Desired Future Performance

Once leaders set the performance criteria, employees need to understand the change program in its entirety. A *change road map*, which details the strategy being used to bring about the change, is a recommended tool for educating employees. Once again it is important that top management make it clear that employee input and help is not only needed, but is essential in making the change process work. An effective road map is highly visible, contains a timeline, and clarifies roles and responsibilities so everyone can see where their input and effort is needed. The main goal of the road map is to allow employees to understand how the company is going to move from its current position to a new, higher level of performance.

Figure 3-1 provides an example of a transformation road map. By not overloading the map with too much detail, this simple yet effective picture helps employees understand the roles and responsibilities of different teams or groups involved in the transformation effort. It also displays a timeline as well as the steps the company will take to realize its vision.

As mentioned previously, unless individuals see a path ahead of them that is manageable and psychologically safe they will often resist change, even if it's in their best interest. But by using a road map you provide the employee with a mental framework of how the company can safely get from point A to point B. This can help the employee see where they fit in and what preparations they might have to make for what lies ahead.

Explaining and communicating the chosen strategy is a much easier task if a large number of employees have been participating all along in gathering industry and company data, as well as helping to set the new direction of the company. When this is the case, leaders need only to reclarify the strategy to those already involved in the change process, freeing up additional time for extensive communication to those who have been less involved in the direction setting and data gathering.

Effectively communicating the change strategy requires much more than holding a kick-off meeting and including in-

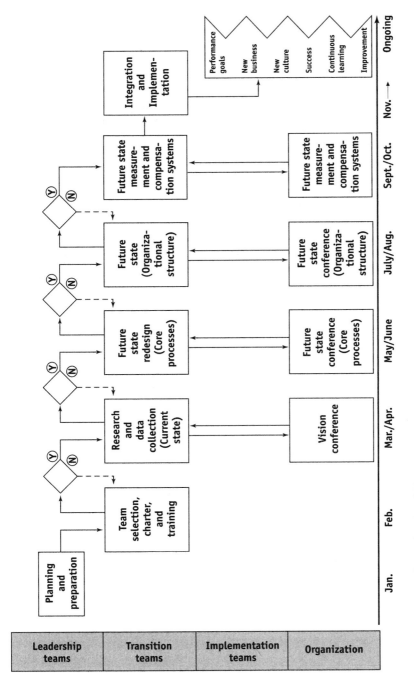

Figure 3-1. A Transformation Road Map

formation about the strategy in the company's newsletter. It means communicating the message in a variety of ways *every single day*. Nor is the communication something that top management can do on its own. Jeanie Daniel Duck, in her *Harvard Business Review* article entitled, *Managing Change: The Art of Balancing,* emphasizes the importance of managers throughout the organization being capable and effective communicators:

> Communications must be a priority for every manager at every level of the company. This is particularly true during a change effort, when rumors run rampant. It is important for the messages to be consistent, clear, and endlessly repeated. If there is a single rule of communications for leaders, it is this: when you are so sick of talking about something that you can hardly stand it, your message is finally starting to get through.[11]

The type, extent, and variety of communication used by President Bill Clinton during the 1996 U.S. Presidential Campaign is very similar to the communication effort required by leaders when launching and leading an organizational transformation. Regardless of your political stance, you can appreciate the drive and determination of President Clinton as he traveled across the country spreading his message. He demonstrated strong leadership characteristics as he went to great lengths to educate, inform, and motivate citizens of all types. He endlessly repeated a clear and concise message to the point where he probably could hardly stand to hear it himself. He relied on not just on television ads, but public speeches, debates, newspaper articles, radio talk shows, and other mediums. Organizational leaders should use this example of presidential campaigning when communicating change throughout their company.

Stage 6: Seek Out and Celebrate Easily Attainable, but Important, Early Successes, and Reinforce Behavior Consistent with Company Values

Immediate and convincing demonstrations of the power and effectiveness of the change program can help appreciably in promoting an attitude of "this stuff works" and "we can do this." Just as important, these early successes, when impacting customers or suppliers, deliver the message that there is a new and better way of doing business. While it is true that an organization will not really transform itself if only small incremental changes take place, it is these small achievements that help to generate support for the more difficult and larger changes that lie ahead. This is why the success of these early change efforts should not be left to chance, but instead should be carefully chosen and targeted.

Targeting these early successes will require organizational leaders to commit a significant amount of time and resources to accomplishing this goal. It should also be clear that those projects with the highest likelihood for success should be chosen. Not only will low-risk, high-probability of success projects most likely succeed, but they will provide change agents with the opportunity to bring what they learned to the more challenging projects still on the horizon.

Fundamental change does not occur right away. In fact, many times employees don't realize the true benefits of a change program for several months, sometimes even years. This makes it even more crucial for leaders to celebrate those small but significant accomplishments that employees have made and that bring the organization closer to its goals. Leaders must even more frequently reinforce employee behavior that is consistent with the values of the organization, regardless of the outcome. This reinforcement, whether it be monetary reward or public recognition, helps to create what Edgar Schein refers to as a sense of psychological safety amongst employees. This not only reinforces positive employee behavior, but also helps employees to change, since taking risks and doing things differently are encouraged, not punished.

Stage 7: Make Change and Continual Improvement a Way of Life for the Organization

Organizational change has no finish line. Instead, as a large-scale change program nears completion, continual improvement must begin in order to sustain the benefits gained during the transformation. Organizations that view their transformed self as requiring no further improvement will quickly fall prey to those in the marketplace that are never satisfied with the status quo. And any chances of sustaining a lasting competitive advantage will quickly diminish over time.

Although organizational change and improvement are never-ending, individuals involved in a transformation must understand that continual change and improvement means improving on what has been redesigned, not constantly changing the structure, processes, and systems of the organization. Changing too much over a long period of time will inevitably lead to confusion, frustration, and chaos. This will not only negatively impact employees but will keep them from focusing their attention on the changing needs and demands of their customers. This is why a change road map is important. If you have a change road map that details the transformation effort, allows employees to see the end in sight, and includes continual improvement as the follow-up to the transformation, it will help to make continual change and improvement a company norm.

Chapter 4 discusses the steps needed to establish a high level of employee involvement within organizations. It will also explain many of the benefits to be realized from empowering the work force.

Tap Into the Potential of All Employees

4

"If an organization aspires to fundamental change, it must change the fundamentals."

—J. Richard Hackman[1]
(Prof. of Social and Organizational Psychology, Harvard University)

Involving employees in each and every stage of the transformation process is an absolute must. Without a form of continual codevelopment between management and workers, the employee resistance to change will often sabotage any large-scale change plans. With this in mind, how can leaders create a work environment that fosters high-levels of involvement from all of their employees? What are the *elements* that truly empower and involve all employees? How do organizations benefit from having an empowered workforce after the transformation process has been completed?

Creating a High-Involvement Work Environment

With so many employees already acting as leaders in their community, managing households, and being parents and teachers to their children, why are most organizations structured on the premise that frontline employees cannot and should not contribute to the "thinking-side" of the company? Quite simply, the answer lies in an out-moded catch-22 attitude of top managers. This is an attitude that says lower-level workers do not 1) possess the information; 2) have decision-making skills; or 3) have the knowledge needed to make the "correct" decisions—the same correct decisions top management can make themselves only because they *do* have access to these crucial areas.

Of course under these conditions managers are correct in not trusting their workers to make the proper decisions. How can anyone expect them to contribute to the thinking-side of the company when their work environment does not give them the following:

- *Access to critical information* needed to make important daily decisions
- *Adequate decision-making skills training* so they can be placed into a position of authority
- *Appropriate authority to make decisions* in their area of responsibility

Under these kinds of restraints no one can make the same kinds of decisions as those who do have information, training, and authority/power.

If these same restraints were imposed in our nation's communities, our country would look very different. Community volunteers could not make even small budgeting decisions because they would not have access to their nonprofit organization's balance sheet or receive basic financial skills training. Similarly, parents would have to seek approval from the town or city government regarding decisions concerning their own children, because even day-to-day decision-making capabilities would be removed and placed in the hands of a small group of senior officials. There would even be restrictions on informal sharing of advice between neighbors for fear that the wrong information would be dispersed, because ordinary citizens would not have the proper knowledge to think, assess, analyze, and make a difference.

This may sound a little extreme, but it is not very different from the culture of some organizations in the recent past. All organizations must reexamine the way they restrict employees from using their full potential. And when companies identify these barriers, they must move swiftly to remove them and allow all of their employees to make the largest contribution they can to the organization.

It Takes More than Pushing Authority Downward

The mistake many leaders make during an organizational transformation is that they push power and authority downward but fail to also provide the necessary training and information that their workers need to make the "correct" decisions. Ralph Stayer, the CEO of Johnsonville Foods, Inc., tells the story of how he made the mistake of going from authoritarian control to authoritarian abdication too quickly:

> No one asked for more responsibility; I forced it down their throats. They were good soldiers, and did their best, but I had trained them to expect me to solve their problems. I had nurtured their inability by expecting them to be incapable; now they met my expectations with an inability to make decisions unless they knew which decisions I wanted them to make. . . . I now see in a way they were right. I really didn't *want* them to make independent decisions. I wanted them to

make decisions I would have made. Deep down I was still in love with my own control; I was just making people guess what I wanted instead of telling them.[2]

Fostering a high-level of employee involvement is about pushing information, decision-making skills training, and power/authority downward to all levels of the organization.[3] In addition, as mentioned in Chapter 2, employees must be educated about their company's vision, values, and strategies. Without this vital education, managers will still be hesitant to hand over decision-making power to employees for fear that their employees will make decisions inconsistent with the overall goals of the company. Likewise, employees will reinforce management's hesitation because they cannot possibly make proper decisions in a strategic context if they are kept in the dark about their company's strategic direction.

Four Elements to Empower Employees

Much has been written about empowering employees— to the point of becoming a cliché— but far too many companies pay little more than lip service to the subject or else give employees more responsibility but little compensation or strategic direction from leaders. Why? Despite all the literature and conferences on this subject, top management still has little understanding of delegation and even little desire to delegate authority/power to fully empower employees. Yet without employee empowerment they will never tap their greatest resource— the knowledge worker. The following sections will more precisely define the four fundamental elements that truly empower employees. The fundamental elements are:

1. Vision, value, strategy sharing
2. Information flow from the source
3. Relevant training
4. Power and authority sharing

As is the case with the crucial elements leaders must establish before launching an organizational transformation, these four employee-empowering elements are intertwined in such a way that a high-level of employee involvement will not be manifested if even one of them is out of alignment or underimplemented.

Vision, Value, Strategy Sharing

Inviting employees throughout the organization to contribute during the initial stages of the transformation phase, i.e., strategic planning, is the best way to ensure that employees make future decisions that are in line with the company's strategy. If an organization is going to put decision-making power in the hands of employees, a shared strategy (with shared values that everyone can relate to and live up to) will replace the need for a detailed list of procedures for how employees or employee teams should handle every situation.

RITZ CARLTON HOTEL. The Ritz Carlton Hotel chain has such a strong customer-service mentality that they allow each and every employee to spend up to $2,000 to correct a guest's problem—without needing authorization. This type of decision making in the hands of all employees is a terrific example of how a culture based on trust and shared values can replace any 1,000-page procedure manual. It is also one of the many reasons that they were winners of the Malcolm Baldrige National Quality Award.

NORDSTROM. Here is another example of a company that uses extensive training and strategy-sharing sessions to empower its employees. In fact, upon completion of the initial training period, Nordstrom gives new hires a one-page "employee manual" that contains just one rule; "Use your good judgment in all situations. There will be no additional rules."[4]

While this type of decision-making philosophy is extremely progressive, understand that companies need to carry out extremely careful selection processes to identify those employees who will excel in this type of environment. Furthermore, regardless of the extent of the training and strategy sharing provided, from a customer's perspective this type of decision-making structure diminishes standardization. While this may attract new customers or retain loyal customers in some situations, it may also confuse and irritate those customers that have grown accustomed to having their concerns handled through standardized procedures.

Information Flow from the Source

In order to do their job effectively, employees need access to all kinds of information. The best type of information is direct and immediate feedback from internal or external customers. Examples include information from customers in the areas of service quality, turnaround time, price, and overall satisfaction.

In traditional, hierarchical organizations, information filters through several layers of middle management before it is finally delivered to the frontline employees. In a high-involvement organization, the information flows from the source, customer, process, etc., to the frontline employees. Such information must be direct, meaningful, and timely. The recent advances in information technology systems greatly assist in this type of direct information flow. Top management should also consider electronic data interchange (EDI), e-mail, the Internet, and many other information-exchange systems, as they all can help facilitate the flow of information to the frontline employees throughout the organization.

Without access to this type of information, employees will have difficulty in better serving their customers or becoming involved in the daily problem-solving tasks that would help an organization to continually improve. As said in Chapter 1, organizations in today's business environment must respond quickly to their customers and constantly foster new ideas about products, services, and processes if they are to succeed.

Relevant Training

Organizations must provide employees with relevant training if they are to acquire decision-making responsibilities, have direct customer contact, or work effectively in a team-based environment. Relevant training must cover the following:

- Basic team training
- Financial analysis training
- Technical skills training

For employees and the company to benefit from such training sessions (as well as many other types of training), the employee must immediately and consistently put these newly acquired skills to use. Merely having a training budget that sends the employees through the motions of learning something without real consequences is wasting the employee's time as well as the company's money.

SOUTHLAND LIFE. This is a company that has implemented a customer-service team structure that is a popular trend in the insurance industry. It is a structure that gives employee teams greater access to more information, coupled with increased decision-making responsibility. A skill-based pay system, in which employees receive increases in compensation as they learn new skills, was established to encourage additional training and skill-building for the members of these teams. Much of the success with the new team-based structure is due in part to the company requirement that at least once a day employees must demonstrate competency in the new skill area for which they just received training. Without this type of consistent new skill use, employees will eventually forget most of their training or make inappropriate decisions when they are required to use these new skills. Additionally, the company loses out because they are spending precious funds on training employees while receiving very little benefit from their investment.

Power and Authority Sharing

What is behind people's desire for power and authority? What drives them into "empire building?" Is it merely the need to control and command—running a tight ship? Is it what a person thinks they should have and do when they own or are responsible for something? Is it purely a persons' natural need to possess what they perceive as their own territory? Or is it simply a result of people's egotism?

Giving up power and authority is probably the most difficult element for all levels of management to share, yet it is the *most* important element for empowering your employees. It is difficult because for decades the old-school, traditional organizations have rewarded and advanced those who oversee big departments and have power over a large group of people. Instead of being rewarded for business results these managers are rewarded for building large departments from which they can oversee and control the largest number of people.

To break this paradigm all levels of management must share decision-making power and authority with employees. A failure to do so undermines the entire empowerment effort. Remember, the whole point of employee involvement (or empowerment) is to create an environment where employees throughout the organization make accurate and timely decisions on a daily basis to best respond to customer needs and desires. Managers from all levels must relinquish and redistribute some power and authority if the organization as a whole is to respond quickly to customers and foster innovation.

How do managers switch from an autocratic to a participative style in order to enable employees to not only share in the decision-making process, but also to make intelligent decisions that can help create a high-performance organization? These four steps form a good start:

1. As mentioned earlier, those employees involved in the decision-making process must have the necessary information and training.

2. Everyone should understand that the time element will often dictate the extent to which different individuals can get involved.

3. Managers must explain that there will probably be some cases in which decisions must come from the top-down; when these situations do arise, it is up to senior management to clearly explain why this is the case.

4. Those becoming involved in the decision making must make the organization as a whole the number one priority, not their own division or department; departmentalization comes from the old autocratic/authoritarian

school of thought of command and control — empire building. The fewer layers of departmentalization (and authorization) in the organization, the more quickly and efficiently you will be able to respond to your customers' needs.

Aside from having day-to-day decision-making power, employees must be involved in decisions that affect their work. At the beginning of an organizational transformation — when fundamental, large-scale changes are being planned for the structure, processes, and culture — employees must be invited to participate in designing and developing the new organization. This is especially important when decisions impact their workplace. Keeping employees from these key activities, yet promising increased day-to-day decision-making responsibility in the future, creates an atmosphere of doubt and indecision, stifling your empowerment and transformation effort before it can even get off the ground.

Benefits of a High-Involvement Organization

Recent research suggests that there is a positive correlation between high levels of employee involvement and both company productivity and long-term financial performance.[5] In particular, data collected from an extensive investigation of productivity in the steel industry reveal that a systematic program for involving employees raises productivity significantly, while the introduction of any one single element has no effect on productivity.[6] Stated another way, to realize financial benefits from empowering the workforce, organizations must involve employees in all aspects of the business. Only asking employees to work in teams, for example, will not improve individual, team, or company performance.

Several different studies indicate the positive relationship between formal employee training and productivity improvements and quality output.[7] These studies underscore the importance of training that provides general problem-solving skills so that employees can respond rapidly to changing market conditions, avoid production delays, and anticipate potential problems.

These studies are a small sampling that supports the mounting evidence that for employees to become truly empowered, top management must push the four fundamental elements downward through the organization: vision/value/strategy sharing, information flow, relevant training, and power/authority sharing. Furthermore, to generate the desired levels of improvement in productivity and overall performance increase, top management must systematically incorporate these four elements. By using the framework established in this chapter, creating a high-level of employee involvement throughout the organization, organizations will tap into the potential of every employee and allow them the opportunity to make significant contributions.

Chapter 5 examines the role employees must play in helping to design and develop the organization of the future.

PART TWO

Transforming the

Work System

Use Transition Teams to Redesign the Company | 5

Part One set the direction for the initial steps that must be taken to ensure a successful organizational transformation. In these early stages much of the initial responsibility falls on the shoulders of top management. Employee involvement during the transformation is essential to creating a successful future organization. What is the best way of getting employees committed to leading the change effort? The use of transition teams is usually the best way. But this statement raises the following questions: What are transition teams? Why should they be used? Who should be on these teams and how should team members be selected? What are their core responsibilities? What kind of assistance do these teams need from top management and internal or external consultants? How should transition teams involve customers and suppliers in their work?

What Are Transition Teams?

Transition teams are groups of individuals from different functions and levels throughout the organization brought together to analyze, plan, and implement changes to processes, systems, and structures. Individuals are usually assigned to these teams full-time for six to nine months. After these teams present their design to a group of senior managers, often called the *steering committee* or *leadership team*, transition team members then rotate into new assignments, return to their previous positions, or become members of the team responsible for implementing the new design.

Most companies undergoing a transformation or large-scale change effort use transition teams as a means to design the future state of the organization. They do so because transition teams bring together people with a diverse set of ideas, experiences, and backgrounds. By forming a small team that is a diverse sample of the organization, companies are able to redesign at a fast pace, yet are still able to think through how proposed changes will affect or benefit the company as a whole.

Why Use Transition Teams?

Managers and consultants working in isolation cannot transform the company by reengineering or redesigning core processes, systems, and structures and expect employees to put the new design to work and make it happen. *The employees whose work will be affected must effect the changes.* No one knows more about the work than those employees who are doing it every day. These are the true experts, and their total involvement in all aspects of the transformation is essential to the creation of a competitive advantage. When organizations realize the goal of tapping into the potential of every employee, they will then sustain that advantage for the long-term.

The failure of most reengineering and other change efforts can be traced back to a lack of employee involvement. Many companies have made the mistake of bringing in consultants to "take over" the change process and then work only with top management. When this happens, employees are kept in the dark about the changes being made around them. Also, by leaving employees out of the decision-making and recommendation process, you further alienate them from the change effort. This approach not only increases the fear and stress level among employees, further increasing their resistance to change, but overlooks the potential contribution employees can make throughout the organization. Without the employee participating and contributing in every way possible, an organizational transformation will never get off the ground and few changes will ever be implemented.

How to Select Transition Team Members

Establishing and organizing transition teams is an involved process. Since transition teams are challenged with the task of recommending fundamental and substantial change companywide, the most respected and brightest managers and employees, specialists and experts, and frontline workers must become active participants on these teams. The companies that fail to put the most qualified and respected individuals on these teams clearly demonstrate that they view the transformation as less than the number-one priority for the company. These companies also jeopardize the outcomes because "the best and the brightest" in the company do not become involved in planning and implementing the changes that will directly affect the company's long-term performance.

ALLINA HEALTH SYSTEM. At the beginning of their transformation effort, this Minneapolis-based, integrated, not-for-profit healthcare provider formed three gap groups to analyze and determine the difference between where Allina is today and where they want to be in the future in three core capabilities: 1) information and knowledge, 2) clinical care, and 3) service excellence. Because Allina sees the transformation effort as one of the company's most significant initiatives, involving virtually every employee over time, they made a concerted effort to select the best and brightest to be members of these gap groups.

One gap group includes a vice president with over 30 years of experience in health care financial management, as well as a project director with an MBA and MHA (Master of Health Administration), whose past experience includes involvement in a redesign effort at another hospital. In addition, this transition team has a registered nurse with a 10-year background in managed care and 10 months of experience on a continuous quality improvement task force, and also another 30-year veteran whose previous position was director of nursing.

Allina Health System has gone to the same great lengths in choosing the members of its Service Excellence Design Team. This team was selected by the Executive Office and is challenged with creating a design and implementation plan for service excellence across the entire organization. The team is chaired by the Allina President and has as its members seven company vice presidents, a director, and a practicing physician. This diverse group not only represents a cross section of the organization but is actively soliciting input from managers throughout the company.

Allina Health System is an example of a company that understands the importance of putting the best and brightest individuals on their design teams. This kind of commitment to bringing together the best possible team will greatly increase Allina's goal of creating a new level of service excellence — a level of health care experience that will sustain a lasting competitive advantage in the health care industry .

Use a Steering Committee or Leadership Team

How companies go through the process of selecting team members varies from company to company. In most cases, the steering committee or leadership team educates employees about the transformation effort and describes the various roles and responsibilities that must be filled by the transition team. Once this is accomplished, employees and managers are asked to add their name to a list of potential candidates if they are interested in working on the team. Steering committees take this information and make their selections, in private, and then recruit additional individuals whom they feel would make a significant contribution to the change process.

Ask If the Best and Brightest Are Aligned with Senior Management

It is important to note that if the "up and comers" in the organization do not volunteer to become members of transition teams, the change effort is not being well received by employees. These best and brightest employees might be resisting because they feel the change effort is doomed to fail, or that top management isn't really supportive of the change plan. If this is the perception, then it is perfectly understandable that these employees are hesitant to link their professional reputation to a change effort. Why would they participate in a plan that looks to be a sure loser, or why alienate themselves from senior managers who aren't buying into the need to change.

This returns us to the need for strong support and leadership from top management, as well as a clearly, intelligently, and relentlessly communicated change strategy that will enable the company, and all employees, to realize its vision. When this is in place, the best and brightest employees will align themselves with senior management and play key leadership roles as members of a team challenged with transforming the company. Instead of keeping their distance, employees will begin to volunteer for positions or assignments that will involve them in different aspects of the transformation.

Include All Employees in the Change Effort

Because transition teams are usually small, ranging from 6 to 12 people, many employees who would like to be members are left out. When you are faced with the situation where the number of people who desire to be transition team members exceeds the available slots, it is crucial that you have those individuals who aren't selected participate in the process in other ways. Never make anyone feel as if their participation is unwanted or that their contribution will not add value to the process.

When an insurance company in the beginning stages of a transformation effort found itself with several more employees than they needed for their transition teams, it wrestled with the problem of how to involve these employees in the change effort without them getting in the way of the transition team members. What the steering committee finally came up with was to involve these employees in the formulation of the companies' vision statement. The Vision Team, as these employees were named, interviewed customers, suppliers, management, and fellow colleagues to gather data about the future of the industry and the company. With help from the steering committee, this team developed a survey and used the data to formulate a vision statement that was accepted by an overwhelming majority of the organization.

Solicit the Viewpoint of Suppliers and Customers

In addition to selecting the right individuals inside the organization to become members of the transition team, customers and suppliers should also be invited to participate in these teams. While suppliers and customers rarely become actual team members, their input is vital because customers and suppliers provide a different viewpoint, one that can be frequently overlooked by those individuals who are too close to the process or system.

RYDER DEDICATED LOGISTICS. This provider of Dedicated Contract Carriage, made the mistake of not inviting customers—either existing or potential—to participate in their initial effort to design a wider range of services throughout the logistics supply chain. Had they solicited customer comments and ideas at an early stage, the design team would have been able to offer more customized services that would have met the needs and wants of its core customers as well as attract potential new customers.[1]

To correct this problem, Ryder invested a significant amount of time and money in customer research and used that information as a starting point to transform their company to meet rising customer expectations. As a result of the new strategic direction and transformation effort, Ryder had a record sales year in all contractual businesses in 1994 and a 40% growth in dedicated logistics revenue in 1995.

What Are the Core Responsibilities of Transition Teams?

The roles and responsibilities of transition (or design) teams during a transformation can vary widely from company to company. Depending on the experience, education, skills, and background of transition team members, a team may be highly autonomous, needing little support and assistance from top management and external consultants. Conversely, those transition teams whose members lack the necessary skills, background, and experience to take lead roles during the transformation will rely more on the steering committee to guide them in the right direction. They will also have to rely on consultants to provide tools, techniques, and tips to assist them during the transformation effort.

Regardless of whether a transition team is composed of experienced and highly skilled change agents or inexperienced but eager-to-learn employees, it is crucial that transition teams gain a sense of ownership during the transformation process. If the steering committee "runs the show" instead of steers, or external consultants take over instead of assist, this will diminish the role of the transition teams. Teams that don't have any ownership and that serve only to make a few minor recommendations to top management will not get seriously involved in the redesign effort. On the other hand, those teams that are empowered to recommend how the future organization should operate, will become more involved. They will also make better decisions as well as develop better solutions.

Here's an example: Chrysler's CEO, Robert Eaton, understands the need to give teams authority and ownership. He, along with other senior executives, meets with new vehicle development teams whose responsibility it is to develop new models or revamp old ones. Together they outline a vision for the vehicle and set aggressive targets. The result is a contract between top management and the new vehicle team. According to Robert Eaton:

> That contract simply sets out all the objectives we hope they achieve. Then they go away and do it, and they don't get back to us unless they have a major problem. And so far, they aren't getting into any major problems. Now, if management became involved with them, inevitably we would give our opinion, and we would get our imprint upon it. It would become Chrysler's vehicle or Bob Eaton's vehicle. But because we stay out of it, it becomes their vehicle, and they work much, much harder, with much more pride, and the success or failure is theirs. As a result, every single vehicle we have done since I have been at Chrysler has come in below its total investment target and its cost-per-car target.[2]

Transition or design teams need to feel empowered like the new vehicle development teams at Chrysler. When they share a sense of ownership and have a charter and a vision to guide them through the change process, they will work much harder because the design of the new company becomes their design.

Similar to when organizations have a difficult time filling slots for the transition teams, it is a warning sign when transition team members distance themselves from the design and refer to it as the steering committee's design or top management's view of the future. If this is the case, the steering committee must turn over more authority to the transition team and allow them to take the lead role in designing the future organization.

In situations like the one mentioned above, it is helpful to have an external consultant working with the transition team(s) and the steering committee to clarify team roles and responsibilities. As a neutral player and experienced change expert, a consultant can be up-front and honest with steering committee members when they are overstepping their bounds or when transition team members need to take on more responsibility. Few transition teams have the expertise to know when or how to confront their steering committee or leadership in the event that the leaders are overstepping their bounds.

With or without the assistance of a consultant, in this type of situation it is important for the steering committee to revisit the charter so that they can reevaluate the roles, responsibilities, and boundaries of each group involved in the transformation effort. (These roles and responsibilities are described in the next section of this chapter.) If the roles and responsibilities have been left out of the charter, the steering committee should put the change process on hold while they, along with the input of the transition team(s), clarify in writing the roles and responsibilities and mission of each team involved in the transformation.

Eight-Stage Transition Team Activity Plan

Though roles and responsibilities of transition teams will vary from company to company, most transition teams take part in common activities during a transformation effort. In this section an eight-stage transition team activity plan will detail the activity stages that most transition or design teams undertake. This plan was developed by the consultants at Miller Howard Consulting Group and has been successfully used in different variations at companies such as Shell Oil Company, Corning Inc., and Allina Health System. These stages can apply to one or more transition teams responsible for redesigning core processes, or to one transition team challenged with redesigning an entire organization.

Following the description of each activity stage is a simple eight-stage checklist (see Table 5-2 on page 93). This checklist was used by the redesign steering committee at Allina Health System to communicate to all employees an overview of the redesign project and the role of the design teams. This was but one example of the timely and credible communication techniques used by Allina to communicate on a regular basis with all employees.

Stage 1: Training, Charter, and System Identification

During this stage, team members undergo extensive training in the different aspects of organizational change. A combination of classroom education, current management readings, guest lectures, and individual instruction with a consultant or change expert, prior to any transition team work, goes a long way toward preparing these members for the challenges that lie ahead.

Understanding the Material

Whenever possible, top management should allow several weeks for team members to absorb and understand the material being presented to them. If you are a reader with a strong knowledge of organizational change, ask yourself how long it took before you became competent in this area. What educational background, seminars, books, articles, case studies, and/or site visits helped you learn about change management, leadership, core process redesign, team building, etc.? How long did it take before you considered yourself knowledgeable in this field? Think about these questions when you are confronted with transition team members who are struggling with different aspects of the change process or who don't seem to be learning fast enough. Be patient and provide assistance whenever possible.

For some transition team members who come to the team with limited knowledge and experience with organizational change, they will be challenged with learning a tremendous amount of information in a very short time. Instead of overloading these team members with every tool or tip during the initial training session, deliver some training at a later date as needed. This advice may seem like common sense, but oftentimes design teams become overloaded with tools, techniques, and tips in the beginning and then are not called on to use these skills until months later. By this time, much of what they learned is forgotten and the consultant or expert who delivered the training is long gone.

Organizations also need to constantly expose these teams to the best practices from outside the company and to knowledge from others who have undergone a transformation. You should encourage transition team members to attend seminars, invite guest lecturers, and make site visits to broaden their knowledge of what it takes to successfully transform an organization. Remember, the more time and resources provided for training and education, the more valuable the contribution these team members can make to the transformation of the company.

Because they will be one of the primary communication vehicles during the transformation, each team member must thoroughly understand:

- The company's new strategic vision
- Why the change is needed
- The scope of the change effort
- The change plan being followed
- The goals to be realized

You should spend extra time with transition team members who have spent prolonged periods of time in only one or two areas of the company. Team members accustomed to thinking about the company in terms of the activities taking place in their previous department or position will take a longer period of time to think about the company as a whole system.

Agreeing upon the Charter

After an in-depth look at the factors that lead to a successful organizational change effort, transition team members need to understand and agree upon the charter that was developed by the steering committee to launch the transformation. The charter is used to define the vision and strategic plan for the organization. It can be thought of as the *Constitution* of the change process and will be referred to by the transition team throughout the transformation. The charter gives clear and consistent answers to questions such as:

- What values do we as an organization embrace that will not change?
- What type of new culture do we want to create?
- What type of competitive advantage are we trying to create in our industry?
- What change plan are we following?

Transition team members need to clearly understand the charter, or else you run the risk of them constantly debating these questions, easily developing different and even contradictory answers to what is stated in the charter. Without a consistent answer to each question, transition teams run the risk of developing systems or process designs that do not align and link with the work of other teams. This problem can occur even when they develop slightly different answers to these important questions.

Viewing the Organization as a Whole System

After training and charter clarification, team members must identify the processes or systems to be transformed. All members must understand these at a master level (or birds-eye view) so that they understand how design changes to one part of the system will affect the rest of the organization. In other words, team members must learn to view the organization as a whole system.

For transition teams responsible for redesigning one core process or system, this means that they need to be in constant contact with those teams redesigning other systems in the organization. This is the key to creating a network of aligned and linked systems. Without ongoing communication between transition teams, impressive and technologically advanced processes and systems may be designed, but you will create inefficiencies and waste when these processes or systems are finally forced to operate together at the end of the transformation. To deliver true value to customers, you must be constantly communicating an overall strategy for aligning the efforts of different transition teams; you must design and link new processes and systems so that when they are finally implemented they operate as part of a whole system.

A whole system viewpoint is especially important, considering our increasing reliance on information technology systems in all aspects of our work. For example, a transition team responsible for redesigning the company's order entry-to-fulfillment process might choose a software system that makes the most sense for their area under consideration. But, without communication with other transition team leaders, the software system selected may not be compatible with existing or future systems. Do not wait until the implementation stage to smooth out the inconsistencies between processes and systems.

Stage 2: Current State Data Collection and Research

Prior to transition teams redesigning a core process or whole system, teams must collect and analyze information so the current state of the process is understood in detail. In Stage 1 it was enough for the team to understand the general overview of the organization. In Stage 2 team members need to meet and interview key players involved in each process to learn all there is to know about that area of the business. Almost always the key players will be those individuals or teams that are closest to the process. By talking with these experts and observing their work, transition team members can learn about the specifics of the process under redesign and can actually see how each component comes together to form the current process.

It is important that the whole process be reviewed and data be collected for each segment. Capturing information on every piece of the process and recording how different individuals do the same job differently will help the team map how the current state varies. This will help identify potential breakthroughs in the future.

While research and data collection may seem like a job that can be passed on to others in the organization besides transition team members, it is crucial that transition team members be the individuals who actually go out and interview people and observe the process in its entirety. If certain team members have personal experience with part of the process or system, they should learn about areas outside of what they are familiar with. The goal is not to have every team member individually gather information about the whole process; rather, the team as a whole needs to have firsthand knowledge and a detailed understanding of the process they are responsible for redesigning.

Identifying Process Performance Indicators

During Stage 2 you should identify process indicators for future measurement. Identifying the indicators that will accurately assess the performance of the process will help transition team members track and measure data to be used for benchmarking in later stages. Another approach to thinking about measurement involves spending time with your customers and suppliers.

Transition teams must keep an eye on their internal or external customers and suppliers as they research and collect data for the current state of the process. If ensuring customer satisfaction remains the overriding goal of the redesign, then you need to have transition team members go out and interview customers. If team members focus on what customers and suppliers like or dislike about the current process or the way the company does business with them, then they will learn about the business from the perspective of the customer. This is valuable information that can be useful throughout the redesign process. More detailed information about diagnosing customer needs will be discussed in Chapter 6.

Stage 3: Process Mapping and Analysis of Current State

The goal in mapping the current state is to define how the process works today. Although information gathered during the research and data collection stage may motivate team members to discuss how different improvements would increase the performance of the process or improve customer relations, the process map must define the current reality.

The purpose of the map is to visually present the current process such that everyone understands how we do business today. Only by clearly understanding the present can we hope to identify opportunities for change.

Four basic types of maps are used by transition teams to define the current state.

1. *Picture map:* provides a macro-level view (or picture) of the process or set of processes under examination in the organization.
2. *State change map:* examines the physical changes that take place to inputs as they are transformed into outputs. The activities involved are not mapped.
3. *Process flow map:* provides a visual explanation of the activities involved in completing the process. It is a simple and easy-to-understand description of who does what activities in what order.
4. *Relationship map:* Describes how work flows among the people involved in the process. Using this map it is easy to see how delays and bottlenecks occur when people must wait for others to complete an activity before they can complete their step in the process.

(For a more detailed explanation of these process-mapping techniques, read Chapter 6 of *Whole Systems Architecture—Beyond Reengineering: A Guidebook For Designing Work Processes and Human Systems for High Performance Capabilities,* Miller Howard Consulting Group, Inc., 1995.)

Current State-Analysis Steps
In addition to mapping the current state, transition teams must also analyze the current state to identify internal and external customers, input requirements, suppliers and vendors, cycle times, tasks and sub-tasks, and costs. Table 5-1 is an example of the steps a client transition team undertook and the information that was collected during the current state analysis of their core process.

Table 5-1. Current State Analysis Steps

1. Define processes	• Macro-level understanding • Key players in process are identified
2. Identify client needs	• Consistent service • Competent/Skilled personnel • Timely service/Minimal downtime • Cost effective/Competitive service
3. Define process input requirements	• Accurate/Complete information • Client/Business requirements • Corrrect/Functional equipment • Timely execution/Delivery
4. Map work activity	• Completed a picture map • Completed a process flow map • Completed a relationship map
5. Analyze problems	• Too many nonvalue added activities • Lack of common systems • Inaccurate data used as input, resulting in increased cycle time • Lack of clearly defined and documented processes • Multiple handoffs • Duplication of work efforts • Poor interaction among service providers
6. Determine root cause	• Roles and responsibilities not clearly defined • Lack of focus on total solution • Fragmented resources across department • No measures of effectiveness, i.e., cost • Client does not understand financial implications • Lack of, and inconsistent use of, systems • Too many silos within different processes • No consistently understood processes
7. Identify opportunities for change	• Install workstations for access to impact problem system in client work areas • Modify the current procedures, and inform affected personnel in writing that only one approval signature is required • Create a balanced scorecard for workstation services • Consider implementation of a workstation structure that includes client-aligned teams (CATs) and a "floating" pool of workstation support resources • Develop a standard process for all workstation deliveries and exchanges

Stage 4: Benchmarking

In Stage 4 members shift from examining the way their process or processes work and turn their attention to how other companies with similar macro processes perform. The intent is not to copy from these companies, but to compare notes about such issues as customer service, cost, cycle time, and so on. You can apply the lessons learned from benchmarking when redesigning processes and systems. This information is invaluable when trying to create a competitive advantage.

As will be mentioned in greater detail in Chapter 6, transition teams should look to companies in and outside their industry. Companies in the same industry often have similar processes in place from which to benchmark, but depending on the level of competition, few competitors will be willing to share their best practices. Opportunities for benchmarking within the same industry will often come from suppliers and/or customers. These organizations frequently have similar processes and are willing to share because their success or failure likely depends to some extent on your company's ability to succeed in the marketplace.

GENERAL MOTORS. One company that is a model for sharing their best practices is General Motors. Through their PICOS Project, a process improvement methodology, they have completed over 12,000 workshops to suppliers, dealerships, Hughes Missile Systems, and most recently the health care industry.[3] PICOS is a Spanish word for mountain peaks. It symbolizes General Motors' determination to become the best in the three key customer satisfaction areas of quality, service, and price. General Motors developed PICOS when dealing with their external suppliers. Forced to reduce supplier costs by 20 percent, General Motors offered these tools to help their suppliers meet their

aggressive cost-cutting targets. After using the process inter-
nally throughout General Motors, the company applied these
tools in their dealerships, proving that the concepts of PICOS
were applicable to the service industry.

Once General Motors implemented and succeeded with the
PICOS process at Hughes Missile and Electromotive operations—a high-tech, low-volume producer—they began ap-
plying the process to their largest outside cost, health care. At
the Sloan-Kettering Institute, for example, the PICOS process
has been instrumental in the restructuring of physician practices, the change of traditional roles and tasks, and in the re-
training of staff—all from a patient-focused perspective.[4]

As demonstrated by this example, companies can greatly
benefit from benchmarking both inside and outside their industry. And as suppliers, dealerships, and even health care
providers associated with General Motors have found out, a
great place to start is those companies with which you currently
have established business ties.

Stage 5: Clean-Slate Redesign

Given the importance of this stage, I have an entire chapter
(Chapter 6) devoted to providing readers with a plan for redesigning and aligning core business processes. As you will
read, the success of the redesign will rest on the transition
teams' ability to design a process or set of processes that creates
a competitive advantage for the company. Supporting structures and systems are then developed so the redesigned
processes can flourish in the new organization. The methodology for developing a new organizational structure and new
systems to support the processes will be detailed in successive
chapters.

Stage 6: Transition Plan Development

After the transition team completes the design stage, their focus switches to developing a plan to integrate the new system with the old. They identify the process owners who will be responsible for leading the integration effort in their area. Then they create separate plans for each process and link them together through a master or macro-level plan that takes into consideration the whole organization.

It is crucial at this stage to immediately develop a transition plan for each process. Delays and downtime will only hinder the transformation effort and keep the design from moving off the paper and being implemented. To avoid this, the steering committee should assist the transition teams during this stage.

While developing a transition plan is a challenging assignment, transition teams cannot become fixated in this state. Presenting a good design and transition plan to the steering committee and moving it quickly to the implementation stage will keep the momentum of the transformation going and will increase the likelihood for success.

Stage 7: Presentation to the Steering Committee

This is the stage when the transition teams prepare and present to the steering committee a cohesive document integrating all the design efforts underway throughout the company. This document should chronologically represent the work of the transition teams during each of the past six stages. It should highlight the most important design considerations, reserving other less important pieces of data to appendices or subsequent binders.

Above all else, the design should be far-reaching, yet realistic. It should stress to the steering committee the need for quick action and the time and resources needed to make the design a reality. For those transition teams that have worked closely and kept in constant communication with their steering committee, the presentation should not be a surprise, but rather a momentum-generating point for those members of the steering committee and transition teams who will rotate into new assignments as members of the implementation team.

Stage 8: Implementation

As noted in the previous stage, not all transition team members move on to become active players in implementing their design. Often, a few team members suffer burn-out while others move on to new positions within the company. This is not all bad. Often the mixture of old and new members brings renewed energy to the difficult task of implementing the design.

The steering team also changes as well. While it does not frequently lose or add new members, it has a new set of roles and responsibilities different from the design period. As is mentioned throughout this book, you need a strong and committed leadership throughout a transformation. During the implementation stage, strong leadership is imperative. This is the moment where employees have to change their behavior — where resistance to change is high as individuals try to cling to the old way of doing things. But with top management support and leadership, all of the hard work of the transition teams can pay off. Though there may be some resistance, the organization is now in a strong position to put in place new processes, structures, and systems that align and link the skills and talents of all employees. With strong leadership and the use of transition teams that helped create the vision, plan the transformation, and implement the changes, the organization can now create a lasting competitive advantage.

Table 5-2. Transition Team Activity Checklist

---

1. Training, charter, and system identification
- ☐ Transition teams receive appropriate training
- ☐ Charter explained and agreed upon
- ☐ System is understood at a master level

---

2. Current state data collection and research
- ☐ Team members meet the process players and key customers and suppliers
- ☐ Information is collected; entire system is reviewed
- ☐ Certain aspects of system are identified for performance measurement

---

3. Process mapping and analysis of current state
- ☐ Team members begin macro-level process map
- ☐ Map is driven by master view
- ☐ Map identifies internal customers, suppliers, cycle times, costs

---

4. Benchmarking
- ☐ Members identify and locate industry players with similar macroprocesses
- ☐ Visit players—compare notes
- ☐ Benchmark data used for a high standard for new macroprocess

---

5. Clean-slate redesign
- ☐ Information is captured and integrated into one flow of inputs, process, outputs
- ☐ Ideal system is devised using a blank sheet
- ☐ Supporting structures are developed to cover system

---

6. Transition plan development
- ☐ Members develop manner in which new system will be integrated
- ☐ Specific processes and their owners are identified
- ☐ Separate plans are created so each process owner sees old versus new

---

7. Presentation to the steering committee
- ☐ Cohesive work document is prepared
- ☐ Other redesigns are integrated
- ☐ Work plan presents a chronology that reflects urgency, yet is realistic

---

8. Implementation
- ☐ Members identify major implementation issues
- ☐ Steering committee roles defined
- ☐ Plan moves from design to implementation

Table 5-2 shows the activity stage checklist used by the steering committee at Allina Health System to communicate to all employees an overview of the redesign project. It clarified the roles and responsibilities of the different design teams. You should consider using a similar list to communicate the transformation plan your company is following.

How Consultants Can Assist Transition Teams

Few transition teams or steering committees undergo a large-scale change effort without the assistance of a consultant or team of consultants who are skilled in change management and organizational redesign. But what is the best way to use consultans? What general deliverables should you expect from them?

When consultants are assisting clients during a transformation effort, the responsibilities of each partner must be clearly defined. The role of consultants (internal or external) is to *facilitate* a transformation process, *not own it*. The vision and changes must belong to the client, not the consultants. If the transition teams feel that the transformation is being done to them, as opposed to them transforming the company, the teams will lose interest and will fail to implement, or will even fight, the changes that the consultants recommend. On the other hand, if they know the consultants are there to assist them in creating the vision, planning the transformation, and implementing the changes—if the employees themselves become the instrument in changing the culture—the organizational transformation has a much higher chance for success.

Consultants facilitate the transformation process by objectively listening to the four voices of the organization (customer, employee, process, and stakeholder) during an initial analysis period. Through interviews with employees, managers, customers, and other important groups, and by gathering industry and company data, the consultants can form a broad picture of the common themes that illustrate the need for drastic change. By understanding the common themes and sharing this information with the clients, the consultants ensure that the organization's change program is focusing on the big picture and is heading in the right direction.

Often companies bring in specialist consultants to redesign an information system or install a new compensation system. This is much different than the management consultant. The list below shows the roles an external consultant normally performs during an organization's transformation effort. An internal consultant or change agent experienced in organizational change, and equipped with redesign tools and techniques, may be capable of performing many of the same activities.

Consultant / Change Agent Roles and Responsibilities
Transfer Knowledge
- Transfer knowledge and skills to the transition team and steering committee members and to internal consultants.
- Bring external experiences and background to the change process.

Assure Readiness for Success
- Continually inform the organization and transition team members about barriers that might prevent the successful completion of the charter.
- Recommend steps for successful implementation.

Facilitate Team Development
- Facilitate the creation of a culture where each individual is a valued member of the team and the team is working interdependently toward the achievement of the charter.

Facilitate the Design Process
- Facilitate the team interactions and keep the teams on course with the chosen change plan.

- Develop straw model approaches and plans and be responsible for administrative and logistics-related decision making.
- Assure "out of the box" thinking and charter fulfillment.

Coordinate Activities

- Coordinate team and sub-group activities to assure linkages and timely completion.
- Facilitate large group conferences involving employees, customers, and suppliers to gather ideas and increase buy-in to the change process.

Facilitate Boundary Management

- Facilitate collaboration among the steering committee, transition team, and key stakeholders.
- Minimize interruptions to the design process.

Communication Progress

- Update the steering committee on past and planned team activities, key lessons, near-term opportunities, and barriers to progress requiring their assistance.

Networking

- Establish and maintain relationships with key subject matter experts and stakeholders within and outside the organization to provide additional expertise to the design process.
- Coordinate site visits to benchmark companies who are willing to share information.

Chapter 6 discusses how transition teams can successfully redesign and align core processes. This is essential to a successful transformation and for gaining a competitive advantage. A four-step redesign process is examined in detail.

Redesign and Align Core Business Processes | **6**

> *"There is a real performance leverage in mov-*
> *ing toward a flatter; more horizontal mode of*
> *organization, in which cross-functional, end-*
> *to-end work flows link internal processes with*
> *the needs and capabilities of both suppliers and*
> *customers."*
>
> —Frank Ostroff & Douglas Smith
> (McKinsey & Co. Consultants)

Central to any organizational transformation is the need to re-design (or reengineer) the core business processes of the organization. As this chapter will explain, top management must generate the support for the changes, lead and assist the transition teams, and stay around for the most crucial stage — implementation. Only by redesigning the core business processes, creating good jobs, fostering teamwork, and making structural changes as well as social system changes can an organization realize long-term performance improvements that increasingly deliver added value to customers.

This chapter will answer these and other questions: What exactly is core process redesign? More importantly, what steps should organizations follow to redesign and align their core processes? What are the roles and responsibilities of the steering committee and transition teams during this stage? What other groups need to be involved?

What Is Core Process Redesign?

Core process redesign (CPR) is starting with a clean sheet of paper and redesigning and aligning the core business processes of an organization to realize dramatic improvements in performance: cost, quality, service, and so on. It is the exact opposite of the incremental improvement of a specific aspect of a process, which usually only serves to temporarily cover-up major weaknesses or inadequacies of the current process.

FORD MOTOR COMPANY. A well-documented example of a CPR (or reengineering effort) was Ford Motor Company's redesign of their procurement process. This included purchasing, receiving, and accounts payable. Ford Motor Company was initially seeking to incrementally improve this process by introducing technology that would, they hoped, reduce head count by 20%. But competitive benchmarking of Mazda's procurement process forced Ford executives to come to the conclusion that what was needed was a total redesign of their process to bring their costs down to competitive industry levels.

Michael Hammer and James Chamy, upon examining the procurement process at Ford before and after the redesign, had this to say in their best-selling book, *Reengineering the Corporation*.

> Ford's old parts acquisition process . . . began with the purchasing department sending a purchase order to a vendor, with a copy going to accounts payable. When the vendor shipped the goods and they arrived at Ford, a clerk at the receiving dock would complete a form describing the goods and send it to accounts payable. The vendor, meanwhile, sent accounts payable an invoice. Accounts payable now had three documents relating to these goods—the purchase

order, the receiving document, and the invoice. If all three matched, a clerk would issue payment. Most of the time this is what happened, but occasionally . . . the documents did not match. The clerks spent the great majority of their time straightening out the infrequent situations in which the documents—purchase order, receiving document, and invoice—did not match. Sometimes, the resolution required weeks of time and enormous amounts of work in order to trace and clarify the discrepancies.[1]

Starting with a clean sheet of paper, Ford Motor Company redesigned the procurement process using new developments in information technology and benchmarking from Mazda (of which they owned 25 percent). They went from having 500 people involved in vendor payment to only 125. The redesign dramatically improved performance and cut costs well beyond expectations. Hammer and Champy explain the new process:

When a buyer in the purchasing department issues a purchase order to a vendor, that buyer simultaneously enters the order into an online database. Vendors, as before, send goods to the receiving dock. When they arrive, someone in receiving checks a computer terminal to see whether the received shipment corresponds to an outstanding purchase order in the database. Only two possibilities exist: It does or it doesn't. If it does, the clerk at the dock accepts the goods and pushes a button on the terminal keyboard that tells the database the goods have arrived. Receipt of the goods is now recorded in the database, and the computer will automatically issue and send a check to the vendor at the appropriate time. If, on the other hand, the goods do not correspond to an outstanding purchase order in the database, the clerk will refuse shipment and send it back to the vendor.[2]

Redesigning all core business processes is not right for every company. As Thomas H. Davenport, head of research for Ernst & Young, says: "This hammer is incredibly powerful, but you can't use it on everything."[3] If certain business processes match-up against world-class competitors' processes or are among the best in the industry, by all means look to continuously improve the process, not tear it up and start from scratch.

But the vast majority of companies are striving to develop *world class* or *best-in-industry* processes. For them, appropriately using CPR offers them the best approach to dramatically improve overall company performance. But core process redesign is not easy, and it can be dangerous. Companies must take care they handle the redesign effort properly, otherwise they are certain to find themselves draining company resources, destroying morale and motivation, and wasting valuable time.

The most important lesson to be learned from those companies attempting a CPR is that no matter how important it is to the success of their transformation, CPR is not an end in itself. A redesign effort is only one part of a comprehensive change plan needed to transform an organization. All redesigned processes will fail to produce the desired performance improvements unless senior management has been making the appropriate changes to the corporate culture. Senior management must also create a new organizational structure as well as new social systems that will support these newly redesigned processes.

In a series of meetings with Harry Moser, Gemini Consulting's Vice President of American Operations, he discussed the importance of doing more than just redesigning processes. In company after company he has seen dramatic and necessary process improvements fall prey to organizational cultures that resisted the change. His experience has lead him to the following conclusion: "Any changes made through core process redesign (CPR) can be undone by culture over time. *Culture is stronger than CPR*."[4] Said another way, in order to realize lasting dramatic performance improvements companies must make changes to the whole organization: process, structure, culture. Solely reengineering processes is not enough to create any lasting advantage.

A Core Process Redesign Strategy

Understanding what CPR is, and when it should be used, is an important first step in the redesign strategy. The more difficult next steps are organizing, planning, redesigning, and implementing the redesign work. Begin by developing a CPR strategy: organizations should view the core process redesign as a part of an overall change plan that is nearly as comprehensive as the organizational transformation itself. In fact, many of the characteristics and stages are the same. The four stages to developing a CPR strategy are as follows:

1. *Organizing and team building:* Top management is responsible for leading the effort and assembling the right group of people to carry out the redesign.
2. *Assessing, communicating, and planning:* To redesign specific business processes, companies must first define customer value, communicate the change imperative to employees, and determine the processes to be redesigned.
3. *Core process redesign:* This stage involves redesigning the process by which the company transforms supplier inputs into customer outputs. Companies should consider starting with a clean sheet of paper and redesigning and

aligning the processes without working under the restraints of the current system. It is a good idea that upon
completion of the redesign, companies pilot their new
process. This will help them pinpoint problems they can
remove prior to implementation.

4. *Implementation:* To maximize and gain the investments
made in organizing, planning, and redesigning the
processes, the company must move quickly to get each of
the new processes up and running. This last stage of the
core process redesign phase is the most crucial as organizational roles and responsibilities change and customers
encounter the new processes for the first time.

We will now discuss these four CPR stages in greater detail.

Stage 1: Organizing and Team Building

On the macro-level, meaning the company's entire process redesign effort, the job of the CEO is to create, and be part of, a
steering committee that develops a new strategic direction and
vision for the company. Once this is in place and a charter is
drafted for the change effort, the steering committee, lead by
the CEO, then selects and assembles the transition team(s) to
redesign the core processes of the organization.

As noted in Chapter 5, transition teams do not immediately
begin to redesign the business processes. Instead, they must undergo extensive training, identify macro-level business processes, gather and analyze data, and benchmark industry leaders.
And they must do all of this before they redesign and align the
processes.

In some cases, companies might assign members of the
steering committee to assist and support the different transition
teams responsible for redesigning the various processes. These

process owners, as they are often called, should not be interpreted as the controllers of individual transition teams. Their purpose is to provide their transition team with resource assistance and leadership and serve as a communication link between the transition team and the steering committee.

To avoid the steering committee members from dominating the transition teams they are leading, it might be more suitable and productive for these individuals to act as resources or coaches for the transition teams. Under this scenario, the company would select the most capable members of the various transition teams to be process owners. This approach avoids a potential power struggle between individual steering committee members and still leaves the communication link between these two groups intact. In any case, you should assess the strengths and weaknesses of the different individuals who might serve as process owners before making the decision regarding which approach best fits your company.

Formulating a Blueprint of Core Processes

It is in this first stage that the company translates the newly created strategic direction and company vision into a blueprint of core processes. Keep in mind that you will be redesigning and linking these processes to maximize your effort at creating a competitive advantage in the marketplace. This blueprint of core processes should be formulated only after the steering committee undergoes a macro-level customer diagnostic phase determining the needs and wants of its customers. By determining the elements that constitute customer value and by taking a quick look at its current capabilities, companies can highlight the processes that need to be redesigned. At this point the company is now ready to create a new set of strategic capabilities.

In essence, this is a strategic planning or capability planning stage. By determining what customers a company is striving to serve, and assessing current capabilities—technological, personnel, financial, etc.—a company is strategically planning for the future. The strategic or redesign plan must also include performance improvement targets that are aggressive and span the entire business unit. A CPR effort that has minor improvement targets or that looks to redesign only single activities or functions will not produce the desired dramatic improvements in performance.

The CEO Must Dedicate Time to the Redesign Effort

The amount of time a CEO dedicates to the redesign effort is a key factor in determining the likelihood for a successful redesign and alignment. He or she must not only lead the steering committee but also visibly and clearly communicate the redesign efforts to employees throughout the organization. To begin consensus building, top management must recognize the need for and act on direct and personal communication to employees on all levels. A series of memos or videotaped speeches from the CEO will never generate the total organizational support needed to lead the company through a transformation effort.

In his article entitled *Keeping Core Process Redesign (CPR) on Track*, John Hagel notes the importance of having the CEO and other senior executives (or business unit heads) visibly engaged in the company's redesign efforts: "How a CEO and senior colleagues spend their time is a powerful signal to the rest of an organization of the priority attached to a CPR effort."[5] Studies vary as to the actual amount of time executives should commit to the redesign effort, but a range of between 20 and 50% of the CEO's time is a good estimate.[6, 7]

Likewise, on the micro-level (meaning a specific business process), the process owner is responsible for leading and assisting his or her transition team. As mentioned in Chapter 5, it is crucial that the best and the brightest people from all departments become active members of the transition teams. If management is assigning their best people to other projects or keeping them in their current position rather than using them for the redesign effort, then it is a clear indication that senior management is not committed to the redesign initiative.

Stage 2: Assessing, Communicating, and Planning

Upon establishing the steering committee and transition teams and launching the redesign effort on a macro-level, process owners must lead their redesign teams through a customer diagnostic phase to determine which key elements of their process determine customer value. Once this phase is completed the transition teams must undergo an assessment of their current individual processes. In addition, both the steering committee and transition teams will continue to communicate the need for change to employees throughout the organization. The combination of these steps will highlight the areas of competitive advantage—what the company is doing well—as well as uncover aspects of the process that fail to satisfy customers. Without this step, the redesign teams will make internal decisions for their external customers based on perceptions, rather than on concrete data that prioritizes what their customers determine to be of value.

Gene Hall, Jim Rosenthal, and Judy Wade, in their *Harvard Business Review* article, "How to Make Reengineering Really Work," discuss how a customer diagnostic phase clarified a company's redesign effort that was headed in the wrong direction:

An insurance company initially thought customers cared about having a broad portfolio of products and knowledgeable service representatives. However, in the diagnostic phase, the company conducted a comprehensive study of customer needs and found that customers cared more about speedy claims processing, an area in which the company was under performing. The reengineering performance objectives reflected this new information, and they saved the company the wasted effort of redesigning processes less crucial to its competitive advantage.[8]

The gaps you uncover between what the company's process delivers and what customers demand or expect, and what other competitors provide, is vital information that senior management must use to communicate the change imperative to employees. Transition teams and employees that have access to the benchmarking results of competitors (and non-competitors), know what the customers are saying, and see the company weaknesses, will understand and be more committed to the changes that must be made to the process. Employees must understand that without drastic changes made to the process, their customers' demands will continue to go unmet, costs will continue to escalate, and quality will continue to fall. Any of these performance deficits may eventually lead to employee layoffs or the shutdown or sale of the business or business unit.

When you have communicated the change imperative to employees and generated the buy-in throughout the company, the redesign teams are now in a better position to set the performance improvement objectives for the process they are redesigning. It is crucial that aggressive targets be set. Without targets that seem difficult—but not impossible—to achieve, the results will likely be only incremental improvement.

Along the same lines, it is important that the redesign teams set performance targets that are broadly defined. Focusing too narrowly on only one performance objective will jeopardize the other elements that may be just as or even more important to the customers. For example, if a company redesigns solely by cutting costs out of a manufacturing process, it may result in encouraging employees to focus too much on cost control to the extent that quality problems arise and overall customer satisfaction suffers. Companies can avoid this by developing a family of measures (cost, quality, service, speed, etc.) for each process and then creating a measurement and compensation system rewarding employees for performance improvements across the entire family. More will be said about redesigning and aligning measurement and compensation systems in later chapters.

Stage 3: Core Process Redesign and Alignment

However tempting it may be for senior managers to begin a transformation effort by simply picking up a blank sheet of paper and redesigning the company's processes, and then bringing in consultants to implement the changes, this is an approach that has never and will never bring about long-term performance improvement. Organizations must take several crucial steps prior to redesigning processes, steps that are discussed throughout the book that will be recapped here.

Table 6-1 is a checklist that is divided into two sections. The left side of the list details the responsibilities of top management or the steering committee, the right side for the transition teams. You can use this checklist as a check-off sheet to ensure that all these activities have occurred prior to undergoing the core process redesign. For your transition teams to design the

Table 6-1. Activity Checklist

Top management or steering committee activities	Transition or redesign team activities
☐ Undergo a company and industry assessment	☐ Undergo training on organizational transformation
☐ Communicate the new vision and change imperative	☐ Meet with the steering committee to ratify the charter
☐ Define the change strategy and communicate specific goals	☐ Research and collect data on the current state of core processes
☐ Draft a charter to guide transition teams	☐ Map the current state at the macro level
☐ Select and assemble transition teams to redesign core processes	☐ Undergo benchmarking to identify best practices

future processes that will create a competitive advantage, these activities must be completed. Any redesign of a business process or set of processes that takes place before these steps are completed will not produce lasting results.

Thinking Outside the Box
Core process redesign requires using the clean sheet of paper approach to redefine the process that transforms supplier inputs into customer benefits. The first step is for transition teams to form a detailed picture of all the components that impact the current process by documenting the process flow. They can accomplish this by tapping into the data compiled during the process-mapping stage — hand-offs, delays, reworks, number of forms used, duplicated efforts, who makes decisions, and functional barriers, for example.

Once transition teams have a clear picture of the current process, they can start with a clean sheet of paper and redesign completely new processes. Realistically there are always constraints with regard to resources (time, capital, people, equipment), meaning the transition teams don't throw out every-thing current and start from scratch. Clearly the most impor-tant job of the transition teams is to "think outside the box" during the initial design stages and create processes that will align and link to create a system that exceeds customer expecta-tions. This means they must have the authority to look beyond current processes, jobs, and business functions.

It is particularly important for the transition teams that are redesigning processes to think outside the box while ignoring constraints on the current process or system, because it gives them a window of opportunity to consider and benefit from new information technology developments. To foster this type of brainstorm thinking, Rod Laird, a partner with McKinsey & Company, urges his clients to do what he calls zero-base infor-mation redesign:

> What you do is take a particular element of the process in a setting and say, 'If we had perfect information instanta-neously available at zero cost, what would you do differ-ently? How would this process look?' Then you back off and say, OK, that's the perfect world. Now, how much of that can we do, at a reasonable cost, with the information technology that is commercially available?[9]

This is exactly what thinking outside the box requires. It in-volves transition teams *not* working within the constraints al-ready placed on the current system. To do so will hinder your teams during the brainstorming stage, causing them to pro-duce a new design that looks very similar to the current system. You will then be cheating your change effort, adding less value to the customer, and certainly falling short of creating a com-petitive advantage.

Just as you cannot ask transition teams to preserve current processes, you cannot constrain them by forcing them to preserve certain jobs or titles that individuals had prior to launching the transformation effort. If some positions are off-limits, then the transition teams cannot start with a clean sheet of paper. If you hamper your teams by holding them to current processes or jobs, then you can expect your performance improvements to be incremental at best.

When transition teams are denied a clean start they are forced to create a process that flows into and out of certain individual's realms of power. If top management insists on making some jobs off-limits to changes, then the transition teams know that top management is asking them to preserve power bases and management positions at the cost of a creating a truly revolutionary design, a design that may ultimately save money and increase the value being delivered to customers.

Similar to transition teams thinking outside the box in regard to current processes and jobs, senior management cannot make certain parts or functions of the business untouchable if they want real change. Transition teams told up-front to outsource nothing and leave most business activities in place because of previous equipment expenditures will only be able to make minor improvements to current processes. If this is the situation, organizations are not really transforming. They are tweaking or adjusting, creating only incremental change.

The question again returns to whether the steering committee is giving transition teams authority to make aggressive redesign recommendations and, upon approval, to implement the new design. If top management does not instill this authority in the transition teams, the company would be better off not undergoing a transformation in the first place. To realize dramatic performance improvements companies need to commit to empowering their transition teams to make "great" choices. Otherwise you are merely wasting the company's capital, time, and energy—resources you could better invest elsewhere.

Information Systems Technology
New technology, especially information systems technology, is maybe the most visible element that enables newly redesigned processes to generate dramatic performance improvements across an entire business unit. Information technology systems serve as the links between different parts of the business that previously remained out of touch and required coordination and communication between many layers of management.

Companies are using many different software systems to integrate different areas of the business. The SAP R/3 is achieving widespread attention for its ability to link all of a business's core processes in real time, using a single software architecture. R/3 is a client/server application from SAP AG, a German-based company. R/3 is a totally integrated system designed for those who want to control all major business processes in real time, via a single software architecture, on a client/server computing platform. According to Karl Newkirk, Andersen Consulting LLP's partner in charge of its SAP practice:

> . . . it hit at a time when companies wanted to get off the mainframe, and when they wanted a complete solution with multinational capabilities to do business reengineering. R/3 did all that, and now, four years later, they're still riding the wave of being the most established product out there to change a business on an enterprisewide basis.[11]

Regardless of the software your organization uses to integrate all its processes and systems, using information technology to simply automate or link existing systems or departments does not go nearly far enough. To create a competitive advantage, you must design, align, and link new value-adding processes to form a network of activities that your competitors cannot duplicate. Your competitive advantage is then sustained by continually improving this network and responding to and anticipating customer needs.

HOME DEPOT. The competitive advantage for this Atlanta-based home improvement retailer lies not just in its low prices or wide selection, but in linking together its network of activities to deliver exceptional value to its customers. By aligning and linking together all its core business activities Home Depot realizes its strategy of providing the best service, selection, and prices to the general public and professionals.

I learned from a presentation given by the Vice President of Advertising for Home Depot some of the different ways this linkage is achieved. For example, each store has on their staffs experienced painters, plumbers, electricians, builders, and so on, in each department. These professionals are given extensive sales and product training to ensure the highest level of customer service. There are also in-house classes on home improvement activities such as installing a tile floor or building a stone patio.

Through information systems technology, Home Depot uses a sophisticated inventory control system that keeps the stores fully stocked, as well as offers the widest selection of home improvement products in the industry. Low prices are maintained through large-quantity purchases that only a company of Home Depot's size can secure from its suppliers. Professional contractors can even call in advance and place orders that will then be filled and ready at the loading dock while they are in route to the store.

Home Depot also spends capital on prime real estate locations and facilities so they can continually build their stores in areas accessible to home improvement professionals and do-it-yourselfers. They use marketing and advertising campaigns to constantly keep the company name in front of customers. Their human resources policies encourage diversity and reward employees when the company does well, which it has been doing since it opened its doors.

But Home Depot's competitive advantage goes beyond relying on aligning and linking the above processes. They have created other Home Depot-unique systems to stay ahead of the competition. For example, Home Depot invests heavily in its employees through educational assistance programs and empowers and trains them to use their judgment to respond to customer's varying needs and requests. It reaches out in the communities where their stores are located by making monetary and product donations as well as by providing time for employees to participate in a wide variety of community volunteer efforts.

By briefly examining Home Depot's processes and values you can see how an organization cannot depend on doing one or two processes well to effectively compete in the marketplace. If an organization is to realize their company's mission they must develop a network of value-adding process that are all aligned and linked. In the case of Home Depot, even when a competitor grabs more market share by sacrificing profits, this type of temporary measure doesn't threaten their competitive advantage. This is because the competition cannot easily duplicate Home Depot's value-adding network of processes and systems—a strategy that continually creates and maintains its position as the leading home improvement retailer.

The Key Is to Redesign and Align All
Six Organizational Components

Certainly new technology, specifically information system developments, is one of the most visible elements that helps newly redesigned processes generate dramatic results in measures such as speed, cost, and quality. But technology is only one of the six key organizational components that a company must analyze, redesign, and align to support and sustain the benefits of a core process redesign effort. The other five components you need to redesign are:

- Creating a new culture based on shared values (discussed in Chapter 2)
- Changing roles and responsibilities by empowering employees and establishing a team-based work environment (discussed in Chapter 3 and Chapter 7)
- Making changes to the organizational structure to support the new processes and teams (discussed in Chapter 8)
- Redesigning performance measurement systems (discussed in Chapter 9)
- Changing to better compensation programs (discussed in Chapter 10)

In a research study commissioned by the U.S. Department of Labor on the effectiveness of high-performance work practices, the evidence indicates that high-performance practices, i.e., employee involvement in decision making, are usually associated with increases in productivity. The study goes on to state that "these productivity effects are most pronounced when such work practices are implemented together as a system."[12] Changing only one or two of the elements, such as teamwork and measurements, will have little or no effect on performance improvement as a whole.

In light of this kind of research and the testimonies from those involved in successful large-scale change efforts, organizations clearly must address all six components if they are to succeed in their transformation. Some of the components, such as culture and empowerment, need to have changes made to them right from the beginning, because they set the foundation for the transformation movement. Other components, such as technology and use of teamwork, i.e., transition teams, are critical elements that organizations must incorporate and utilize during and after the actual redesign. The last elements—natural work teams, structural changes, performance measurements, and compensation—can only be examined and aligned with the rest of the change effort when the redesign process nears completion and an organization has a clearer picture and better understanding of the support requirements for the new processes.

Piloting The Redesign Process
Once you complete the redesign of the process on paper, you should consider piloting the process before implementation. "Piloting offers several advantages," says Curtis E. Songer, the leader of Deloitte & Touche's National Reengineering Development Team. "It helps to identify potential weaknesses in the process, allows those who will be involved in the process to offer improvement suggestions, and helps to get the bugs out of the IT systems."[13]

Piloting also does two other important things. First, it more precisely clarifies the types of skills and training employees will need to make the process run efficiently. This allows additional training and education to take place before the new process is up and running. Second, a pilot allows those employees who have still not bought into the changes to get a firsthand view of the benefits derived from the redesign effort. Listening to and incorporating the contributions made by these particular individuals is an excellent way to turn these employees (or managers) from pessimists into proponents of the changes.

If your organization decides to run a pilot of the process before implementation, be careful that you don't get stuck in this stage. Use this stage to identify bugs and other weaknesses, and make your changes quickly. The success of the new design depends on what gets implemented, not on what gets piloted.

Stage 4: Implementation and Execution

During the implementation stage the resistance to change will be high because employees will also need to change their behaviors on a grand scale—the old ways of doing things, the status quo, will no longer be there for them to fall back on. Employees are not only filling new positions with newfound responsibilities, but the old power and authority structure will have changed as well. Because of the intensity of the changes, senior management's leadership and support is absolutely essential at this stage.

The CEO and implementation teams must spend additional time and resources communicating the vision throughout the organization. To reduce the fear and resistance, these leaders should continue to communicate on an interpersonal level, using a variety of methods to reach employees at different levels and different facilities. In addition, companies should begin the implementation as soon as possible so the employees quickly can see the benefits of the changes.

Besides communicating to employees, companies should deliver a well-thought-out message to customers so that they have an understanding of how the changes will benefit them. This is especially important when processes have been redesigned that change the way customers interact with the company. It is important to let them know that many of the changes are a result of customers providing your design teams with suggestions at conferences or in other settings. Inviting customers to look at the new process and to ask questions is a good way to communicate to them that the company is serious about meeting and exceeding customer expectations.

Project Management
Recent advances in project management software have made implementing large-scale changes more manageable and more successful. Project management, as defined by the project management consulting firm Young, Clark & Associates, "is a set of generic concepts, principles, and structured techniques by which projects can be: 1) clearly defined, 2) thoroughly planned, and 3) persistently controlled during execution; to successfully achieve project objectives."[14]

Given the complexity of implementing a large scale redesign, I recommend you work with a project management expert to develop a project management system. Referring again to the project management experts at Young, Clark & Associates:

> A project management system is an integrated set of planning and control techniques, policies, procedures, computer software, report formats, project databases, and communication technologies that is designed to support the application of project management by trained, committed, and technically knowledgeable personnel.[15]

The time and money put into a project management system is a worthwhile investment. Considering the size and scope of the implementation effort, and the cost incurred, organizations should invest in a system that provides the implementation team with the tools and techniques it needs to implement the new design. Implementation teams can expect to benefit from the investment in a project management system. A project management system will:

- Communicate up front the roles and responsibilities of all players to avoid schedule conflicts and downtime
- Improve the communication and the ability of the implementation team to work together
- Generate plans and schedules that will guide the team throughout the implementation effort
- Match resource availability to the workload to eliminate bottlenecks in the implementation process

All of these benefits will lead to saving time and will help the organization begin to reap the benefits of their new competitive advantage sooner rather than later.

Note that realizing initial improvements is a key to sustaining the long-term commitment needed to see the redesign effort through from beginning to end. The short-term gains also help to fund the future change programs the company must undertake to completely transform.

Following implementation, organizations must make changes in the way they organize employees and structure the organization in order to realize drastic performance improvement. Chapter 7 stresses the importance of creating "good" jobs and organizing employees into "natural" work teams.

Establish "Natural" Work Teams

> *"To achieve high quality, an organization must achieve optimum output from its people. It must create a system in which people learn, are motivated, care about their work, and seek continuous improvement. High performance is the purpose of teams."*
>
> — JENNIFER HOWARD
> (VICE PRESIDENT; MILLER HOWARD
> CONSULTING GROUP, INC.)

With a newly created network of value-adding processes comes a new set of tasks and responsibilities. To deliver value to customers an organization needs to effectively complete these new tasks. One of the best ways to accomplish this is to establish natural work teams.

Two important questions surface in establishing natural work teams. They revolve around job creation and team design. Specifically, what can organizations do to make sure they create "good" jobs for all employees? And what elements are needed to make "natural" work teams successful? The context of the terms good and natural will be described in this chapter.

Creating Good Jobs

The redesign of an organization's core business processes will not realize dramatic performance improvements unless you create good jobs for all employees. Creating good jobs is about giving employees work that is challenging, interesting, and motivating.[1] Additionally, employees need to receive information, training, and power/authority to enable them to make the appropriate business decisions. Also, each employee must understand the company's goals and objectives and realize how his or her work contributes to the success of their team, and the success of the organization.

ROCKWELL INTERNATIONAL — TACTICAL SYSTEMS DIVISION. Following their core process redesign, Rockwell International made some drastic changes to the quality of work life for their employees. Before 1987 frontline employees had narrow job assignments, little responsibility, and little or no flexibility on how they could perform their jobs. To quote an internal quality consultant who has been with the company for more than 20 years, "Employees were checking their brain at the door and being told how to do everything."[2]

After receiving extensive training, participating in the company's redesign, gaining access to companywide information, and being trusted with decision-making responsibility, frontline employees at Rockwell International are now responsible for setting budgets, performance targets, and scheduling requirements. In addition, employees now have a clear understanding of how their performance impacts customers and the organization as a whole. The improvements to the quality of work life, coupled with the process redesign, explain the dramatic improvements in productivity and product quality over the past several years. As mentioned in Chapter 1 these improvements increased Rockwell's shipment of missiles from 11 per week to 28 per day.

Tap into the Potential of All Employees and
Maximize Their Contribution

One of the best ways to maximize employee contributions is to organize them into teams that have ownership of a process or subprocess, and link the team with an identifiable customer(s). Without identifiable customers, teams lose a sense of purpose and have little opportunity to receive feedback that would help them make targeted improvements to their work. In the cases of teams responsible for processes that do not deliver products or services to external customers, it is essential that internal customers be identified. For long processes involving many teams, organizations should identify a series of internal customers to create a customer-focused process from beginning to end.

Figure 7-1 highlights the difference between a process with one perceived end customer and a process with several identifiable internal and external customers. Notice the increased number of feedback opportunities the teams can receive and give in *process B* of Figure 7-1.

How to Establish Natural Work Teams

Simply putting a group of employees together to serve a customer will not create a natural work team. It won't even guarantee a high-level of team performance. The term natural work team as used in this book implies that a process, subprocess, or activity contains a set of tasks or responsibilities that can best be accomplished by using a team or teams of employees. Unlike the theory of scientific management developed by Frederick W. Taylor, which broke down work activities into simplified and standardized pieces so management could oversee and control every aspect of employee work, natural work

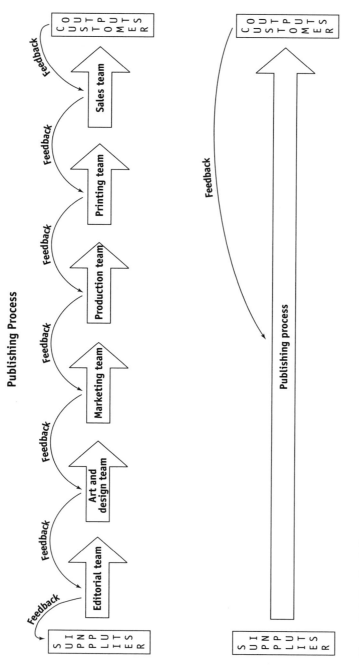

Figure 7-1. Feedback Processes

teams are designed to give employees *ownership* of a complete or whole part of a process. This natural team-based work environment ensures that teams of employees throughout the organization are given direct responsibility for delivering value to customers.

This structure has two unique benefits. First, it pushes decision making downward to the employees who are closest to the customers. This utilizes the talent and skills of employees throughout the company, and when combined with a system of process changes, almost always leads to increases in customer satisfaction. Equally important, this structure frees up management to focus on the longer-term strategic issues that are often delayed when management becomes too involved in running the day-to-day operations of the business. (Chapter 8 will examine the changing role of senior and middle management and the additional steps needed to rebuild and maintain the organizational structure.)

UNION PACIFIC RAILROAD. Union Pacific Railroad established natural work teams throughout their organization by creating permanent, cross-functional National Account Teams for all large customers. (Note: Not all natural work teams are cross-functional.) The employees on these teams are completely responsible for satisfying their customers. The National Account Team for Boise-Cascade, for instance, includes employees from operations, marketing, logistics, finance, and billing. This cross-functional team works to completely satisfy their customer, Boise-Cascade, with regard to all of the services Union Pacific Railroad provides to them. Since the National Account Team was created for Boise-Cascade, the improvements in customer satisfaction have been impressive. Boise has increased Union Pacific Railroad's customer satisfaction rating by three to four points in an industry survey (the survey ranking scale is from 1 to 10).[3]

Pushing decision-making downward to employees who are closest to the customers and giving them ownership of all or part of the process is only the first phase in creating natural work teams. What is needed for these teams to grow and prosper in your organization is the support of a *team management system*. Without a fully aligned and linked management system that continuously supports these natural work teams, the team structure will unravel and all but disappear. To survive and prosper, natural work teams need to have in place the following eight team management system elements:

1. Senior management support
2. Effective team leaders
3. Coaches to support the team leaders
4. Team training
5. Specific performance targets
6. Clearly defined responsibilities for ownership
7. Access to necessary information
8. Ongoing team performance evaluation

Three additional aspects of your organization need to change if you are to deliver the highest value to your customers. They are 1) changing the organizational structure to support the natural work teams, 2) designing a new performance measurement system, and 3) linking compensation and rewards to team performance. These will be discussed in greater detail in subsequent chapters.

Element 1: Senior Management Support

Senior management must look toward natural work teams as the primary building blocks for performance throughout the organization. Therefore, it is the responsibility of the CEO, senior executives, or business unit heads to allocate resources for team development and to change the measurement criteria to include, and stress, team performance over individual performance. Furthermore, senior management is responsible for working with the natural work teams to specify the goals and objectives they are to accomplish. This is an extremely important point because a team lacking proper guidance from senior management can easily lose focus or else concentrate on objectives that are less crucial to the organization.

While senior management must be involved in communicating the goals and objectives to the work teams, it is important that they do not become too involved in their daily work. As mentioned earlier by the CEOs at Chrysler and Johnsonville Foods, teams do not benefit from their senior manager's daily involvement. Teams become de-motivated and lose a sense of ownership when top management talks about the importance of empowerment but fails to truly deliver it.

As will be discussed in greater detail in the next chapter, the role of middle management must change with the development of a new team-based organization. Companies cannot afford to have managers serve solely as communication links and information exchangers between senior managers and frontline employees. Not when information technology systems, such as e-mail, the Internet, EDI (electronic data interchange), or companywide intranets can communicate and exchange information faster, with fewer errors, and at lower costs.

Element 2: Effective Team Leaders

A team leader's central responsibility from the outset is to help natural work team members gradually assume responsibility and control over their own work. So in the beginning, team leaders will need to be more heavily involved in the day-to-day work of their team. Down the line this will not be necessary. The team leader will be free to focus on the coordination and planning for a number of teams.

Of all the team leader's main responsibilities, none is as important as working with management and the natural work team members to develop clear and precise performance objectives—objectives that will serve as the team's guiding light. Creating a team-based work environment that improves morale is a positive outcome, but the primary objective of natural work teams is to accomplish goals that cannot otherwise be completed by individuals working in isolation.

Team leaders must also create a trusting environment both among the team members and with the team leader. This can be very difficult and usually takes some time to accomplish. So team leaders must understand that while trust can only be built over time, it can be lost overnight. In addition to the responsibilities mentioned, leaders must keep their natural work teams focused on performance goals, help them overcome interpersonal distractions, and help them learn from their mistakes. To develop these skills, team leaders need assistance. As mentioned in the next section, coaches (usually internal or external consultants) can provide team leaders with the help they need to succeed in their new roles.

Element 3: Coaches to Support the Team Leaders

Team leaders, especially ones who are new to this role, need a coach to help them with their leadership responsibilities. Expecting a new team leader to demonstrate leadership skills such as listening, giving positive feedback, sharing information, and promoting team behavior without coaching and training from an expert is unrealistic. This would be like expecting a newly drafted college quarterback to make the jump to the pros and lead his team without receiving any assistance or coaching from professional coaches (usually former players)—coaches who know the ins and outs of the game from their years of experience. Just as professional sports teams would never do this to their players, organizations should never do this to their employees.

Good coaches know their goal is to help their team leaders learn the skills and develop the competencies they need to the point where they no longer need full-time support. When the coach's current team leader demonstrates appropriate leadership skills and shows proof that his or her natural work team is competent in several areas, the coach is then free to move on to assist other team leaders.

One of the first areas in which natural work teams must demonstrate competency is the capacity to work effectively together. This includes:

- Sharing responsibility for team performance
- Giving and receiving feedback
- Actively listening to one another
- Handling conflict
- Solving problems as a team

The coach must also be confident that the team leader has the skills to ensure that his or her natural work team can operate effectively without their full-time assistance. Team leaders must also make sure that their team understands its purpose when making decisions. If team members cannot state their mission or objectives, or describe how their activities align to the organization goals, it is a clear indication that the team leader needs additional coaching.

Being customer focused and having performance measures in place to track customer satisfaction and identify opportunities for improvement are two additional natural work team responsibilities. New team leaders should rely heavily on their coaches for assistance when initiating customer contacts and developing measures to monitor their team's performance. The best way to measure a team's performance is to graphically represent their progress and display these scorecards. This way they can be constantly updating and reviewing customer satisfaction. Coaches should make sure that these teams not only have scorecards in place, but that they know how to use the information to identify problems. Natural work teams should also know how to use continuous improvement tools such as process mapping and root cause identification to solve these problems.

Element 4: Team Training

Along with ongoing support for the team leader, team members need initial and continual training to develop and maintain the skills they need to operate effectively. Team training gives team members an opportunity to develop and refine the skills they need to assume more responsibility and control over their own work. Depending on the skills and experiences of the different teams in your organization, training for natural work teams should include a mix of the following:

- Technical skill development
- Business skill development
- Group or interpersonal skill development

Technical Skill Development
Technical skills training should be task specific, such as teaching natural work team members how to use a new software

package, operate a new piece of video-conferencing equipment, or search and retrieve data from the Internet. With companies increasingly using web sites and intranet systems to communicate information, they now can encourage their employees to use home office information systems to link to the office. For example, sales teams could electronically process customer orders at home. The only way to guarantee that your employees have the skills necessary to utilize constantly evolving technology is to continuously provide them with technical skills training. Most employees need more than a few days of computer software or systems training to give them the skills and confidence they need to switch from their current ways of doing things to the newest information technology systems and software. It is best to customize training classes to different employee needs, and develop a plan to help them manage the transition from the old way to the new way. If employee resistance to change remains high, and you have given them the time and opportunity to learn, you should establish a system of consequences that rewards those employees who do learn and change while penalizing those who do not.

Business Skill Development

Business skills involve teaching team members accounting, finance, and entrepreneurial skills so they can assume responsibility for accomplishing such tasks as setting budgets and developing profit and loss statements. The goal here is to educate the natural work team members so they can manage their piece of the process as if it is their own business. Teams that can manage their part of the business make wiser decisions and rely less on management's daily involvement. This reduces costs, frees up managerial time, and improves customer responsiveness.

Some natural work teams, after undergoing business skills training, spin off their services into separate units that operate externally from the company, competing in the marketplace for the same or additional business. Most often, these new company spin-offs provide improved services to their former employer, at reduced costs, while still generating a high return to investors. Despite few employees or equipment changes, these new companies frequently improve service delivery while reducing costs. This is because they operate as true business owners and as educated business owners they realize that bureaucracy and waste affects their company's profitability. They understand that their business must be based on a competitiveness that entails quality, innovation, service, or speed; otherwise their profits will suffer badly. Whereas in the past employees had the luxury of overlooking a bad year for the department because the company as a whole had a good year, business owners are now an island unto themselves.

Group or Interpersonal Skill Development

Natural work team members need education and practice to operate effectively in a team-based environment. Redesigning processes and organizing employees into natural work teams will create a competitive advantage only if you provide employees with the assistance they need to make the transition to a team structure. Most employees will be eager to take on more responsibility and control over the work delegated to them in this new structure. Nonetheless, this type of large-scale change, regardless of whether they perceive it positively or negatively, is stressful to many employees. Companies must realize that education and training helps employees reduce their stress level and overcome their resistance to operating in a natural work team environment.

This is why consulting firms usually recommend specific training that addresses the interpersonal aspects of a team-based culture. Miller Howard Consulting Group, for example, offers a 3-day team seminar that devotes 2 days to addressing issues related to helping employees making the transition to a natural work team-based organization. Class topics include managing and tracking team performance, holding effective meetings, learning team decision making, and resolving team conflicts. Mock team meetings and decision-making scenarios allow participants to prepare for real-world situations in their office. When employees participate in this type of natural work team training it helps them develop the skills and build the confidence to succeed as members of an empowered team.

Regardless of the type of training involved, training is most beneficial when team members clearly understand what skills they will be learning and how these will help them to perform better as a team. For example, claim service representatives, who were formerly secretaries at The St. Paul Insurance Company, underwent formal training in the areas of insurance coverage, customer service, and team management skill development. Representatives understood from the beginning what skills they would be learning and how these skills would assist them in providing better customer service and increasing overall work productivity. As a result, team members greatly benefited from the training, as indicated by their quick ability to handle their new responsibilities.[4]

A more general aspect of natural work team training should be to help team members understand how their outputs contribute to the operations of the company as a whole. Allowing team members to see their work activities from their suppliers' and customers' perspectives can help bring more meaning to their jobs. This understanding of how their work fits into the larger context of the organization helps natural work teams make changes in how they receive inputs and transform them into outputs—changes that will be more suitable to their suppliers and customers.

Element 5: Specific Performance Targets

Senior managers, team leaders, and natural work team members must all be involved in the creation of performance targets that the team will be responsible for accomplishing. But before they arrive at specific performance targets, it is useful to develop a mission statement for each of the natural work teams. A mission statement will help ensure that all team members have a shared understanding of the purpose of their team. Furthermore, mission statements outline a common theme around which the team can rally.

You can develop a clear and shared mission by having all individuals involved answer specific questions with regard to why their particular natural work team was formed in the first place. John H. Zenger, Ed Musselwhite, Kathleen Hurson, and Craig Perrin, in their book *Leading Teams: Mastering the New Role,* recommend using the following questions to stimulate discussion: "What has our team been formed to do? How can we add value to the organization? What would customers say our purpose should be?"[5] These and other similar questions will get team members thinking about their purpose and how they can work together to accomplish their mission.

After the creation of a mission statement, you must develop specific performance targets or goals for the work teams. The general statements commonly found in mission statements, such as "becoming world class" or "providing the highest levels of customer satisfaction," are used to motivate and guide teams. These statements do not make it clear to team members what is expected of them. Performance targets, on the other hand, are clearly defined. They are usually customer-oriented performance measurements that the natural work team knows they are responsible for accomplishing.

For example, an oil and gas company has a mission statement that they want to become an industry leader in oil and gas resource exploration. To help accomplish their goals, they have their exploration teams track the following business measures so they can track and monitor their performance:

- Actual time required to find drillable locations
- Actual time required to update field studies
- Time from lease purchase to drillable status
- Actual time from lease purchase to drillable status
- Number of leases acquired
- Finding costs
- Net barrels from drillable site

By developing scorecards for each measure, benchmarking the competition, and identifying and making needed improvements to the process, this team can fulfill its mission of being the leader in oil and gas exploration industry. If these specific measures were not in place the team would have little direct evidence of the success or failure of their efforts.

Element 6: Clearly Defined Responsibilities for Ownership

The natural work teams being created to accomplish specific objectives must be responsible for their performance. To ensure this, you must allow teams ownership over their work activities. Just as a lack of support from senior management can endanger the team development process, too much intervention or influence from management will ultimately shift responsibility for ownership away from these teams.

When management begins to assume responsibility and control from the teams, team members quickly realize who is making the decisions, so they start to assume lesser responsibilities and contribute in a less meaningful way. The most likely result is that the natural work teams either disband, or they remain in place as purely symbolic gestures that give the impression to outsiders that the company operates in a team-based management style. Organizational performance measures will be the best indicators as to whether teams are actual natural work teams or just facades kept in place by top management.

Boundary Issues Between Management and Teams
To avoid over-involvement by management, boundaries must be drawn to clearly define the responsibilities of the different groups in the organization. Just as a charter was used to define roles and responsibilities during the transformation effort, organizations should draft natural work team charters for their management and team members to refer to when questions arise regarding ownership and responsibility. Don't wait for problems to arise to write a team charter. This will delay the natural work team development process and foster tension between management and employee teams.

Figure 7-2 depicts three scenarios that can occur with regard to boundary issues between management and natural work teams. As illustrated, organizations want to avoid situations A & B, where an overlap (A) or a vacuum of power (B) occur, and create a balance of power, as shown in situation (C).

Element 7: Access to Necessary Information

Natural work teams need access to all relevant information if they are to perform to their potential. This means information

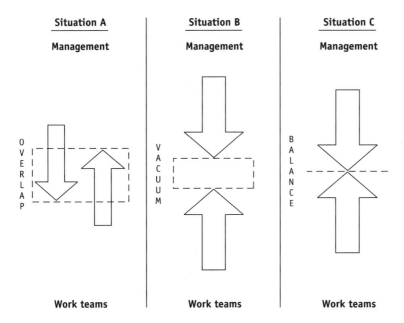

Figure 7-2. Management/Team Communication

concerning customers, suppliers, the industry, and the organization as a whole. This is why an organization must establish information systems that deliver different types of information to the various work teams that exist throughout the organization. The information must be timely, relevant, and unfiltered if it is to assist the team members and increase the value of the work being performed.

Natural work teams should also be key players in developing the information systems they will need to perform to their potential. This is not to suggest that team members should become software programmers or systems experts, but that their input should be solicited throughout the development and installation of the system. This returns to the central theme that runs throughout this book. *Those employees whose work will be affected must effect the changes.* Those closest to the customer and who are living and breathing the work have valuable information. It is this type of human information a company must tap into if it ever hopes to design a future that creates a competitive advantage—a future that the employees accept and want to deliver on.

CHASE MANHATTAN. When Chase Manhattan decided to refocus and redefine the type of company they should be and the type and variety of services they should provide, they quickly realized their information technology infrastructure had to be reengineered. This led to many questions concerning what the new information system should look like and how it should perform. Ultimately, they answered these important questions by examining the information needs of the end-users (individuals and teams) scattered around the world. By focusing on the needs of the end-users they developed a new information system that placed timely, accurate, and useful information in the hands of those people who needed it the most. Says Craig Goldman, Chase Manhattan's CIO, "Our goal (was and) is information self-sufficiency, getting information to the right people, in the right place, at the right time."[6]

Element 8: Ongoing Team Performance Evaluation

Management needs to make periodic assessments of all natural work teams to determine how well they are performing. Regardless of whether a team has just formed or is maturing into a self-managed natural work team, management must get a sense of how well the team is doing in order to give assistance and direction when necessary. When there are no periodic evaluations, or if management is not taking them seriously, teams that are showing signs of trouble will fail to receive help from management—because no one is listening.

J. Richard Hackman, Professor of Social and Organizational Psychology at Harvard University, suggests that a manager or team leader ask three questions when reviewing how well a team is doing:

> First, does the product or service of the team meet the standards of its clients—those who receive, review, or use the team's work? Second, is the team becoming more capable as a performing unit over time? Third, does membership on the team contribute positively to each person's learning and well-being?[7]

By addressing these aspects of the natural work team during an evaluation, a manager or team leader will come away with a clear understanding of how well the team is performing, how fast the team is improving, and how much learning is taking place among the team members.

In addition to top-down evaluations, natural work team members need to keep score in order to know how well they are performing. As mentioned earlier, without a scorekeeping system team members have no way of charting their progress. They will be unaware of opportunities for improvement or situations that call for necessary corrections. Stated another way, teams without a scorekeeping system have no way of continually improving, resulting in them adding less and less value to the organization over time. Chapter 9 will give a more detailed description of creating and using scorecards.

Chapter 8 explains the changing role of middle management and the additional structural changes that an organization must make to support the newly established work teams.

PART THREE

Transforming the Human System

and Sustaining the Change Effort

Build a New Organizational Structure | 8

> *"Relationships are the pathways to the intelligence of the system. The more access people have to one another, the more possibilities there are. Without connections, nothing happens. Organizations held at equilibrium by well-designed organization charts die. People need access to everyone; they need to be free to reach anywhere in the organization to accomplish work."*
>
> —Margaret Wheatley and
> Myron Kellner-Rogers[1]
> (authors of *A Simpler Way*)

The challenge during this stage of the transformation is to design an organizational structure that best supports the newly established natural work teams. A traditional vertical or pyramid structure, built from the top-down, with functional silos (i.e., departments with walls around them) in place, will not give work teams the necessary tools to create a competitive advantage. To improve their performance and continuously add value to the organization they need access to information, colleagues, management, and customers.

This means organizations need to tear down the old, steep hierarchy with layers of management control and put in place one that allows employees to learn, share ideas, and experiment. This is what leads to organizational improvement. To foster learning and sharing, the new organizational structure must be flatter—a more horizontal structure that identifies knowledge and information sources and opens up channels so all employees gain access to each other. Structural change is one of the most difficult aspects of an organizational transformation. This is because like core process redesign organizations must redesign and rebuild in a new, and often completely different way. In the first part of this chapter we will look at four key principles to help build this new structure.

Rebuilding the organizational structure is perhaps the most significant challenge since it involves redefining the roles and responsibilities of those who had the power under the old structure, especially middle and senior management. It is commonly said that these employees have the most to lose during a transformation. It is true that as teams are empowered, taking on more responsibility and ownership, fewer traditional middle management positions are needed. Still, there are a variety of positions and opportunities where these managers can add value and win in the new organization. This will be discussed in the second part of the chapter. I will also look at the changing role of senior management during and after the transformation. Similar to middle managers, senior managers experience concern about loss of power. They face a halted advance up the career ladder due to leaner structures and must concern themselves with having to handle new roles and responsibilities requiring cross-training and new skill development.

This section will examine ways in which to communicate the positive aspects of the transformation and also will emphasize the importance of extensive interpersonal communication between the leaders and their senior management resistors. In addition, I will discuss senior management's responsibility to sustain the competitive advantage by continually refining the company's strategic direction and leading ongoing change.

Move Toward a Flatter Structure

When most people think of the word structure, specifically organizational structure, they envision a clearly drawn organization chart that identifies the CEO, vice presidents, managers, supervisors, and employees, all in their respective departments. Frontline employees are thrown into small boxes on the bottom of the page, while individual middle and senior managers get larger boxes, with their own name, depending on their place in the pyramid. There are lines going from top to bottom, indicating the power structure and flow of command. It is neat and orderly, but what does this tell us?

This type of structure usually only tells us a few things— who makes the most money, who you must say yes to, and who you can delegate work to. And in case you forget, it will tell you what department you are in and how many layers of management separate you from your department's VP. How people do their work, who they go to for information or advice, or even who they share ideas with, is not indicated on this organizational chart. Looking at the organizational structure on paper makes you ask: So how does work actually get done?

In practically every organization there exists an informal structure, or network of relationships, that enables employees to navigate the hierarchical structure to obtain valuable and timely information. This is the information they need for making daily decisions, making process improvements, and providing customer support. This is how the work gets done. When this informal structure collapses or breaks, as it does when a poorly planned employee restructuring changes the structure of these informal networks, the work usually grinds to a halt. This work will not return to full speed until a new network of relationships is established and the right information is placed in the hands of the people who need it the most.

Companies must do away with the traditional structures that solidify power bases and management control while creating obstacles for employees who need access to one another. Instead, they must create new, flatter, less hierarchical structures based on the goal of getting the right information in the hands of the right people at the right time. Because work teams will serve as the foundation for this new, flatter structure it is important to revisit the principle that was established in the last chapter. *The work activities identified during the core process redesign can best be completed by teams of employees who have been given the proper training, information, and authority and who are held responsible and rewarded for their results.*

Another important principle to revisit was discussed in Chapter 5. *The employees whose work will be affected must effect the changes.* Ignoring this principle when building a new structure ultimately leads to those at the top creating a design that sends information and control up to them, while sending commands and directives down. It is the top-down perspective all over again.

To build a new organizational structure that opens communication channels, builds on existing relationship networks, eliminates functional barriers, and empowers work teams to realize their potential, organizations must incorporate four key principles into their design. These principles are:

1. Build the structure around processes, not functions
2. Give work teams ownership of a substantial piece of the process

3. Do not separate the "thinkers" from the "doers"
4. Expand employee skill-bases to increase team problem-solving capabilities

Principle One: Build the Structure Around Processes, Not Functions

During the process redesign stage you need to identify and completely redesign the core processes of the organization. Then you can establish natural work teams as the primary method to accomplish work activities. After this stage it is necessary to change the structure of the organization to allow your work teams to deliver value to their customers—value that is not hindered by a functionally and hierarchically structured organization.

The new structure, therefore, must be one that is built by using the core processes and work teams as the foundation. You add support layers, pools of experts, or management positions to the organizational structure only when you determine that these additions provide value-added services to the teams, and hence, to customers. Layers of management, groups, or individuals that do not provide value do not become part of the structure. This only increases your costs and will lead you to a common problem in organizations today—information overload. By designing the structure from the bottom-up, as opposed to the top-down, you can eliminate the unwanted accumulation of data and information that flows down through the structure. This will then free the work teams to focus on the information they need to get the job done.

At Rockwell International's Tactical Systems Division, for instance, the old organizational structure held the various directors, such as Finance or Engineering, solely responsible for the activities within their given function. "What happened," says

Larry Coleman, with Total Quality Systems at Rockwell, "was that internal empires were created within each of the functional areas. As a result, the focus switched from the product and the customer to the activities within the functional areas controlled by the directors."[2] This in turn caused a swell of information requests by directors and their counterparts to gather and distribute information to justify their position in the organization.

The present situation, after the transformation at Rockwell, has the various directors acting as resources for the cross-functional project teams (work teams) that exist throughout the company. These directors send and lead the teams through training, establish customer contacts for the team members, and work with other directors and the project team facilitators to coordinate the activities and information flow between the various project teams. In this structure teams are not flooded with information requests, requests that distract them from their objectives. Instead they have directors and project team facilitators working in unison to support them in the attainment of their goals and to increase the value they add to customers.

Principle Two: Give Work Teams Ownership of a Substantial Piece of the Process

For the new organizational structure to support natural work teams in adding value for their customer, organizations must remove their functional silos. But even with the removal of functional silos a steep hierarchy may still be in place. To flatten the hierarchy, you must give the work teams ownership of a substantial piece of the process. The greater the scope of ownership the teams have and the greater the reliance on information technology systems, the less hierarchy is needed to link together the activities of these teams. With this new, flatter hierarchy in place it will become clearer how the activities of each support group are linked together and how they are delivering increasing value to their customers.

In BellSouth's Northwest Atlanta District, cross-functional Customer Service Teams have been established to accomplish the work in this district. These Customer Service Teams have ownership of a complete process—phone line installation, for example—and they are responsible as a team for reaching their performance objectives. Not only is the new structure meant to exclude functional silos, but the design plans call for a hierarchy that will be flatter because it will add layers or support groups only after it is determined that they will actually add value to the teams.[3]

This structure is successful because the teams determine the information and assistance they need to complete their work. If it was left up to management to design the structure for the district, the likelihood would be high that the Customer Service Teams would need to establish their own informal structure, or network of relationships, to find the best way to get the work done.

Given the increasing costs and complexity associated with information technology systems, organizations cannot afford to create structures that serve as obstacles that employees must navigate around to accomplish their work. Instead, organizations should be investing their financial resources to build structures developed by the teams that open communication channels and increase interaction between employees who need to share ideas, information, and best practices.

Principle Three: Do Not Separate the "Thinkers" from the "Doers"

Another means to minimize the hierarchy is to do away with the notion that managers are the "thinkers" and employees the "doers." In its place should be a new philosophy that states that those closest to the work (or closest to the customer) know best how to improve the process, handle problems, and satisfy customers.

When organizations fail to incorporate this new philosophy, structures remain in place that reinforce the belief that problems should not be handled at the frontline level. With this kind of tunnel vision, problems must be pushed up several layers in the hierarchy to be solved by the "more competent" manager—a thinker. In this inefficient and ineffective system, the typical manager is so far removed from the problem that he or she wastes time and energy trying to come up with the solution. The problem frequently ends up being tossed back and forth between managers until a final solution is reached, a solution that when it completes its journey back down through the hierarchy often does little to solve the actual problem.

In one sense, combining thinking and doing into every job makes everyone in the organization knowledge workers. This mandates that everyone is required to think, learn, and perform their work. This increases the rate at which the company can improve and creates an environment that values the human intelligence of all employees. This is in sharp contrast to companies of the past that made it clear to their frontline employees that they are supposed to work, not think.

Principle Four: Expand Employee Skill Bases to Increase Team Problem-Solving Capabilities

As natural work teams gain a greater scope of ownership and assume managerial activities in addition to their nonmanagerial work, the employees on these teams must continually expand their skill bases in order to increase their problem-solving capabilities. Unless all members on the teams continuously learn new skills, the team cannot continuously improve or make progress. Worse, they will fail to adapt as new technologies and competitors change the business environment. Furthermore, these untrained teams will need a steep hierarchy in place because they will require management to perform the activities they are not capable of assuming.

Cross-training is a perfect example of the means by which employees can learn new skills in the workplace. A Georgia-based insurance company, Southland Life, for example, provides their employees with training sessions that help them to learn certain skills in a skill set. These skill sets represent building blocks toward total process competency. The knowledge and skills gained in these training sessions allow employees to gradually assume greater responsibility and decision-making capability, which ultimately leads to better customer service and performance.[4]

While you should require multiple-skill learning throughout the organization, it is important to understand that you still need functional experts in some areas of the company. A tax law expert in the accounting department, for example, would most likely not benefit from the same training as customer service representatives. The key is not to remove all of these experts in the organization, nor send everyone through the same training, but rather to encourage functional experts to share their knowledge with those teams that will benefit from it.

To make this possible, natural work teams need to have these experts identified and have communication channels established so that they can quickly learn a new skill or solve a customer problem. Without these established networks, the teams will lose valuable time locating an individual or group to lend the needed assistance. This results in customer delays and lower overall customer satisfaction.

People Pockets

The rehabilitation department in an Atlanta-based hospital developed a unique system to formalize what used to be an informal communication network. *People Pockets*, as it is called, is a file that contains documentation on each therapist's unique set of skills. In the past therapists were assigned to incoming patients on a random basis. They relied on informal relationships to ask for specialty assistance like in the case of neurological traumas. New therapists, or contract therapists hired to meet short-term demands, were unaware of the each therapist's skill sets so they had difficulty finding needed specialty assistance in a timely manner.

Today, when needed, the hospital therapists refer to the People Pockets file to locate and gain expert assistance from therapists skilled in a particular area. This reduces patient waiting time and increases therapist utilization rates. It also maximizes the use of therapists' skills. And when rehabilitation therapists receive certification in a new skill area, their file is updated to reflect their new competency so everyone can use them as a resource.

Changing Role of Middle Management

Traditional middle managers have been and will continue to feel the squeeze between empowered employees taking on management responsibilities and executive levels reducing head count to become lean and more responsive to the changing marketplace. The growth and use of powerful information technology systems has given organizations the latitude to remove middle management levels without breaking down communication between the top and bottom of the organization. In fact, the communication is usually better under this new structure since the information exchange flows uninterrupted and unfiltered between sender and receiver.

In addition to internal changes driving the reduction in middle management positions, external changes in the way organizations conduct business with suppliers and customers have eliminated the need for many positions as well. Through electronic data interchange (EDI), private satellite communication systems, and electronic payment methods, organizations like Wal-Mart and Procter & Gamble have minimized the number of managers needed to collect data from suppliers, distributors, and customers. This means that former managers who once visited suppliers to get monthly reports or who called on distributors for point-of-sale information are no longer in demand. In their place are sophisticated information technology systems that instantaneously deliver data to individuals throughout the organization. Figure 8-1 illustrates how organizations have turned onto their sides and switched from having managers be the sole points of contact to having employee teams receiving data and communicating with their supplier or customer counterparts.

New Roles for Middle Management

I have identified many of the key reasons why traditional middle management responsibilities like supervising, delegating, and transmitting information can be accomplished by other more effective and more efficient means. So what is there left to do for middle management? What role can they play in a company that is constantly seeking to become leaner and flatter?

Of course there are many ways former middle managers can succeed in a newly transformed organization. If it is becoming an internal consultant or a facilitator helping to lead the transformation effort, or if it means taking on strategic

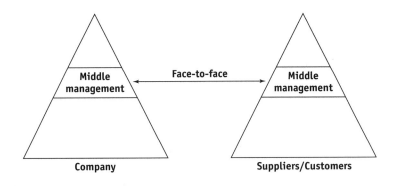

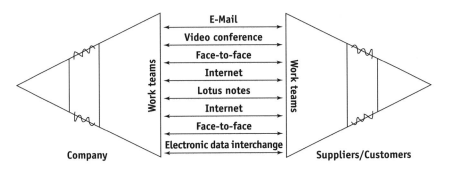

Figure 8-1. Turning the Organization on Its Side

roles to help identify new market opportunities, former or existing middle managers must relentlessly strive to find ways to add value to the organization. As one middle manager at Rockwell International told me, "Although my title or job may change, as long as I add value to the company there will always be a position for me."

The following lists details five new roles or jobs that middle managers can prepare themselves for in order to add value in their newly transformed company:

1. Change agent
2. Internal consultant

3. Process owner
4. Specialist/Expert
5. Knowledge manager

Many of these positions have overlapping responsibilities and are frequently defined differently from one organization to the next. Use this list as a general guideline and assess your organization's needs before positioning for a particular job. The point to keep in mind is that managers, senior and middle alike, who continue to add value will always have a place in a newly transformed organization.

Change Agent

One of the best opportunities for former middle managers is to become involved in and help lead the organizational transformation effort that is underway. As a change agent you can help effect change in the company, as opposed to letting change happen to you. You will also learn new skills that can assist you in finding ways to add value after the change effort is implemented. You will also develop competencies that you can bring to other organizations undergoing similar change efforts.

As an agent of change your core responsibility will be to educate employees about the transformation effort underway in your organization. Whether you participate as a full-time member of a transition or design team, or lead a benchmarking project, you will be asked to present complex ideas in a manner your listeners can understand. You will need to work with a diverse group of organizational members, ranging from senior management to suppliers to work teams, and align and link everyone's effort in a coordinated fashion.

To prepare for this role and succeed you will need a strong knowledge of change management. Whenever possible gather all the information you can about topics such as leadership, transformation, strategy, and teams. Interview colleagues in other companies who are involved in a large-scale change effort. Participate in external site visits and attend seminars and conferences to develop your knowledge. Search the Internet for information. Read books, case studies, and journal articles. Consider a part-time MBA program to come in contact with others who are eager to learn and share their unique set of experiences related to organizational change.

Whether you sense a downsizing effort on the horizon or are currently unemployed, treat this knowledge-accumulation process as a part-time or full-time job. This means setting goals to read a certain number of articles or books per month or making plans and following through on expanding your network of colleagues who will share their experiences or help you gain access to change agents in their company. Your increased understanding of organizational change will be valuable as your company or a future employer realizes the need to transform in order to survive.

Internal Consultant

Internal consultants often wear many hats and provide a variety of services. For the purpose of differentiating internal consultants from change agents, strategic thinkers, or technical experts, I define internal consultants as individuals who use a variety of skills and tools to provide *soft consulting* to team leaders, teams, and management. By soft consulting I mean providing assistance in the areas of interpersonal communication, group facilitation, and team meetings, to name a few, as opposed to technical or financial consulting.

For internal consultants, the challenge is to educate and communicate the importance of creating and/or maintaining an organizational culture based on trust, open communication, honesty, direct and immediate feedback, and learning for all. This education/communication will take place in a variety of situations ranging from one-on-one coaching to facilitating and debriefing team meetings. Regardless of the situation, internal consultants must continually reinforce the appropriate cultural behaviors themselves. As role models they must lead by example. The more traditional and old school the organization the more difficult your task will be in leading a change effort. You will be facing managers and supervisors who may be slow in seeing the personal and financial benefits of creating a new organizational culture.

To effectively educate and communicate, internal consultants must have strong verbal, written, and interpersonal communication skills. Listening actively is by far the most important requirement for effective communication. In addition, internal consultants need confidence to give direct and honest feedback to peers and senior managers regarding their behavior in team meetings and other workplace situations.

Strong communication skills and confidence are but two of a long list of skills and requirements that internal consultants need to demonstrate in order to succeed in their role. Others include self-motivation, assertiveness, credibility, persuasiveness, and a desire to learn and teach. Because few managers are naturally strong in every category, initial and ongoing skill development is necessary to add increasing value as an internal consultant.

Process Owner

As described earlier in this chapter, managers at Rockwell International have successfully made the transition from functional directors to process owners. Their success, and the organization's, is in many ways the result of switching from a narrow functional view of work to a whole systems view. A process owner must have the capacity to understand and manage the interactions of a complex system or process. This requires the ability to interact with a diverse set of suppliers, customers, and teams. Through these interactions, process owners gain a whole systems perspective and use this knowledge to coordinate and align the activities of teams throughout the value-delivery process.

Organizations are most successful when process owners continue to find new ways for natural work teams to learn from each other, their suppliers and customers, and world-class performers. By providing the time and resources for information sharing and benchmarking, process owners increase each teams' ability to make improvements to their piece of the process. Though there will be isolated process improvements that are necessary and valuable, process owners must communicate with their counterparts to coordinate improvement efforts throughout the organization's value-delivery chain. When a company engages in coordinated efforts like these on an ongoing basis, they put a greater distance between them and the competition.

Failing to coordinate process improvement efforts jeopardizes the company's competitive advantage. Organizations also suffer when process owners hoard information and resources in an effort to strengthen their power base. If a work team is having trouble acquiring the information and assistance they need, or is finding it difficult to coordinate their improvement efforts with other teams, it is a sign that you need to replace their process owner. It is important to find an individual who understands and practices the art of open communication—sharing information and resources. Otherwise team performance will suffer as the team members will be forced to devote valuable time looking elsewhere for the information they need to perform their jobs.

Specialist/Expert

For a long time now organizations have been searching for individuals who are both generalists and specialists. Without suggesting that an organization can overlook the importance of having individuals with strong general business and industry knowledge, individuals with strong specialist skills, particularly in technology-oriented businesses and international markets, are in greater demand.

Whether you are a software company struggling to find someone who can provide needed technical expertise to a team of programmers, or a consumer products firm looking for an individual to oversee the development of a new international product launch, experts are hard to find. Internal experts are also in demand because they save companies money that they would otherwise have to spend on contracting a consultant for valuable, but expensive and usually limited consulting sessions. A manager with general experience and strong specialist skills can position themselves as an expert who can add value in a variety of ways.

Becoming a specialist/expert requires you to be proactive. Assess your current skill set and interests, and seek out assignments that will help you develop the new skills and knowledge you will need to succeed in a new role. Don't wait until a new position opens before you begin thinking about the skills or training you might need. There are those who from day one have been thinking long-term, developing the skills and acquiring the knowledge to find ways to add value.

Say, for example, you are a regional manager in your company's marketing department. U.S. and Canadian market share has been slipping for years due to market saturation and intense competition. As a result, your company has plans to pursue international markets. You have heard that plans are in the works to allocate 25% of the entire marketing budget to a new international marketing group, reducing U.S. marketing head count by one fourth. From discussions with colleagues and management it looks as if some time next year the plans will go in effect and they will be launching marketing efforts in two international markets, South America and East Asia. What do you do?

As a proactive individual you do not wait until layoffs are near and limited international opportunities are announced. Based on your skills and personal interests, you should acquire the necessary knowledge to further develop your skills so you can be a key player in the marketing effort to be launched in South America. In addition to your current responsibilities, you research South American economic trends. Through conversations with the VP of Marketing you have learned about the significance of the Brazilian market, so you spend the next several months developing a strong knowledge of Brazilian purchasing patterns for your industry. You develop a working knowledge of Portuguese in evening classes and schedule your next vacation to Rio de Janeiro instead of Paris. You also volunteer to work on a team that will develop a draft of the new marketing campaign that will be presented to top management. Now, when the time comes for international marketing positions to filled, these value-adding activities will put you in a far better position to get the job.

Knowledge Manager

Organizations for some time now have been competing based on their ability to create, collect, and transfer knowledge. From health care providers to consulting firms to aircraft producers, the organizations that create, collect, and transfer knowledge the most effectively are able to lower costs, increase quality, and respond faster than the competition. Given the increasing impact of knowledge on sustaining a competitive advantage, there is an increasing demand for individuals who can manage the creation, collection, and transfer process of knowledge. As discussed earlier in this chapter, organizations need to replace traditional structures with new structures that facilitate open communication, information sharing, and learning. Otherwise you will be relying on old structures to create, collect, and transfer knowledge, structures that will flood the system with useless information that is of no value to your teams. This will eventually block the delivery of valuable information to those that need it to perform their work.

As a knowledge manager you can expect your main responsibility to be the creation of a knowledge management system that has as its goal getting the right information in the hands of the right people at the right time. This will require technical competency and an understanding of the needs of end-users of the knowledge management system. You can increase your technical competency by familiarizing yourself with the software products that allow groups in remote locations to communicate, store, and share information electronically. These software programs—known as groupware, and increasingly the Internet and intranets—have facilitated the development of these knowledge management systems.

A large component of knowledge management is differentiating between what is valuable information and what is useless data, so that information overload does not occur for the end users. Once the knowledge management system is up and running this will be your main responsibility. Clear company guidelines should be in place to clarify what constitutes valuable information. As mentioned earlier, the end-users of the information should determine most of this, so their input should be solicited during all stages of the knowledge management system development.

The foregoing is not intended to detail all of the new opportunities for former middle managers. But these five job categories should provide you with a starting point from which to further examine the new ways in which you can add value to the organization.

Restructuring Senior Management

As noted from the outset of this book, a successful transformation effort requires strong executive leadership and vision. Considering that the organizational transformation described in this book centers around the dismantling of bureaucracy and the empowerment of employees, then it is no wonder that many senior managers resist change and fail to embrace this vision. For those leaders embracing change, but who are faced with resistance from their colleagues, it is important to repeatedly state the case for action as well as communicate the new opportunities that are likely to arise.

Unlike the first two chapters, where I discussed the main responsibilities of leaders at the beginning of a transformation, this section examines the changes senior managers can expect to face as their part of the organizational structure is rebuilt.

Similar to many middle managers, many senior managers experience stress and resist the change effort. Often they perceive the transformation as doing little more than removing their power bases, halting their move up the corporate ladder, and forcing them to take on new responsibilities and learn new skills.

To counter the resistance of senior managers slowing the progress of the change effort, those embracing the transformation must relentlessly communicate and educate their resistors. This ongoing communication should frequently be in the form of data or figures that demonstrate the financial value of empowering others and transforming a company. Senior managers typically warm-up to hard figures that they can pass on to their peers. Additionally, the communication and education must involve detailed discussions concerning the new ways in which these managers can continue to rise and succeed in this new environment.

Spiral Staircase to Success

In describing to senior managers the ways in which they can continue to rise and succeed in the future organization, one should be optimistic, yet realistic. The new organizational structure will call for a leaner executive group, but this does not mean across the board head count reductions are necessary. These managers must come to realize that with fewer top management positions, going straight up the career ladder is no longer feasible. Nor is this approach the way a company should be grooming senior managers to fill the very top management positions.

Instead of a career ladder, I suggest that career growth be viewed as a spiral staircase to success. As illustrated in Figure 8-2, the old career ladder offers a narrow range of positions and assignments, usually in one functional department. On the other hand, the spiral staircase offers senior managers a wide variety of roles and responsibilities that truly prepare them for the top positions in the organization.

Many companies that have embraced the rise of functional managers through traditional career ladders have felt the ill effects of making lifetime functional specialists responsible for an entire organization. In particular, Ford Motor Company during the 1960s and 1970s suffered as a result of the overwhelming dominance of the "finance people" over the manufacturing and engineering managers. The finance people at Ford became the company's elite group. Their department became *the department* from which decisions and orders flowed. The senior executives were almost all finance people with little knowledge of, nor concern for, issues relating to actually manufacturing the automobiles. Their focus was on the numbers and making Ford's stock price rise.

During these critical years in the U.S. and international auto industries, senior manufacturing people at Ford had few board members and little or no power to influence the company's strategic direction. Their requests for capital to reinvest in their plants went largely ignored. The finance people directed the company and requested changes that would make the bottom line look good, regardless of the long-term consequences on the company.

As David Halberstam remarked in *The Reckoning*, his epic tale of the clash between Ford Motor Company and Japan's Nissan:

(Ford's) research and development were chopped back because they were expensive and cut into profits and hurt the way the company looked on its books. Since labor costs were

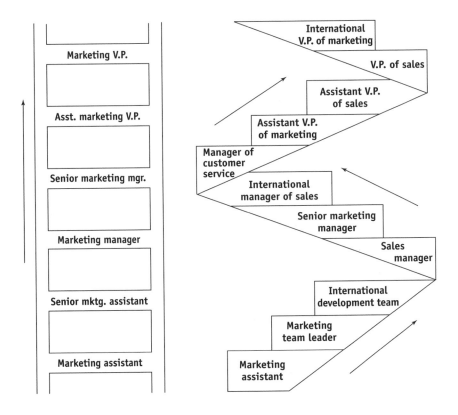

Figure 8-2. Career Ladder versus Spiral Staircase

constantly rising, the reductions were always accomplished by subtracting from innovation and product and factory maintenance. The impulse of product, to make the best and most modern cars possible, was giving way to the impulse of profit, to maximize the margins and drive both the profit and the stock up.[5]

Had senior executives at Ford risen up through spiral staircases that assigned them to positions in manufacturing, engineering, sales, and marketing, as well as in finance, these executives may have made decisions that considered the whole company's long-term performance, rather than short-term results that looked good to Wall Street.

Choosing Senior Managers Who Are Walking the Talk

When leaders are preparing to select individuals to fill the positions in the newly designed structure, it is crucial that they choose only senior managers who have demonstrated behaviors pledging support for the company's new values and culture. While no one expects the attitudes and habits of senior managers to completely change overnight, the organization will suffer tremendous setbacks if newly assigned senior managers do not embrace the company's values. Even a small group of destructive senior managers can undue much of the progress that was realized during the transformation.

In the event that senior managers are not "walking the talk," meaning their behaviors are running counter to what has been deemed acceptable and appropriate in the organization, action must be taken to remove these individuals. For those senior managers whose performance and behavior are both poor, dismissal is automatic. In the other direction, managers who have demonstrated the appropriate behaviors, but have low performance ratings, should be given every opportunity to improve their performance before being reassigned or let go. The most difficult situation involves managers who have a history of strong performance but a track record of behaviors that do not fit with the new culture. When one-on-one coaching and training fails to bring about changes in these particular individuals, they too must be let go.

As Tom Willard, an internal consultant at Shell Offshore Inc. likes to say, "these types of individuals were not fired, they self-selected themselves out of the organization." Whether it is through self-selection or firing, letting these strong performers go sends a clear message to the rest of the organization that behavior that does not support the new culture will not be tolerated—even if you have a good performance history. This decision, although difficult at times, will pay long-term dividends as all organizational members start to realize the financial and personal benefits of employee empowerment and a culture based on trust and communication.

Long-Term Focus, Ongoing Refinement of the Strategy

Through the empowerment of frontline employees and the transition of middle managers into change agents, specialists, internal consultants, knowledge managers, and process owners, senior managers can now focus on their main responsibility: the company's strategic direction. As I noted in the outset of this book, the goal of the transformation is to create a competitive advantage in the marketplace by aligning and linking the whole organization in pursuit of the company's vision. As the transformation nears completion and continuous improvement becomes the focus of the teams, senior management's responsibilities will shift to continually refining the company's strategy and leading change initiatives that further develop and sustain the company's network of capabilities.

Without a long-term focus, an ongoing refinement of the strategy, and continuous improvement, the organization in a sense stands still, allowing competitors to eat away at their competitive advantage. If complacent for too long, the company's once dominant position in the market falls prey to competitors focused on overtaking the industry leader. Instead of standing still, organizations need to set barriers against the competition. A well-planned, executed, and implemented transformation effort, followed by continual improvement, provides a strong barrier against competitors attempting to compete in the same market.

Chapter 9 examines the importance of creating a new performance measurement system that gives teams and individuals the feedback they need to continually improve their performance.

Develop a Performance Measurement System $\quad$ 9

> *"The overall purpose of a measurement system should be to help a team, rather than top managers, gauge its progress."*
>
> —CHRISTOPHER MEYER[1]
> (AUTHOR OF *Fast Cycle Time:*
> *How to Align Purpose, Strategy,*
> *and Structure for Speed*)

Traditional measurement systems, solely focused on functional outcomes and overall financial performance, fail to provide the natural work teams with the necessary feedback they need to improve their performance. As I noted in the previous chapters, to sustain a competitive advantage you must have continual improvement throughout the company. Consequently, it is important to design a new performance measurement system that continuously measures team progress and team performance in addition to the overall financial performance of the company. This is the only way teams can continuously succeed in delivering increased value to their customers, and the only way management can track the return provided to stakeholders.

Developing a new performance measurement system is not difficult if an organization has properly designed and established new processes and natural work teams. This is because the measurement system needs only to measure the natural results of the teams. It is when the processes are complicated and when the teams are lacking structure or ownership of a large part of the process that you run into difficulties. Additionally, a new performance measurement system can become difficult to implement if employees view the new measurement system as a means by which top management can better monitor and control their behavior.

So how does an organization go about developing a new performance measurement system that helps natural work teams gauge their performance? Who should be involved in developing this new performance measurement system? How extensive should this measurement system be? What can management do to ensure that the work teams exercise proper discretion, while making sure they do not control the employees? How do you develop a system that balances the need for information relating to long-term strategic issues and short-term feedback for teams?

The Traditional Measurement System

In the traditional organization the measurement system was developed with three main principles in mind:

1. To measure functional outcomes
2. To measure overall financial performance
3. To control the workforce

Under this reactionary system, the company gathered information and sent it upward through the managerial layers to inform top management of the activities of each functional area. Top management then analyzed the information and sent directives down to the functional directors to increase market share, lower product costs, cut the marketing budget, or improve quality, depending on the functional area being scrutinized. The functional directors then issued the same directives down to the middle managers under their command, who in turn passed these orders down to area supervisors, who at last delivered the message to employees.

The central problem with this system is that it failed to give the frontline employees specific information on how they should go about improving their performance or where they needed to focus their improvement efforts. In a sense, employees were being asked to play the game, but they were not allowed to track their performance or keep score. Management controlled the information and would sometimes let employees know the score at some point in the future, often weeks or months away. More often than not the score was announced to them in the form of a threat to improve performance or face dismissal. Under this system employees throughout the company did not know whether they were doing well, nor did they know what they needed to change in order to improve their performance.

Individuals and teams need the responsibility of keeping score, otherwise they will lose interest in their work — motivation and morale suffer. In the absence of specific feedback concerning their performance, employees could not, nor did they have the desire to, proactively make process improvements, improvements that would ultimately benefit the company. It is no wonder that many companies operating under the traditional organizational model fell victim to competitors who early on realized the value of providing their employees with performance feedback and empowering them to make ongoing improvements to their work.

A New Performance Measurement System

Under the new performance measurement system, companies have their newly established natural work teams gather the feedback required to help them continually improve their performance. The new measurement system also empowers teams to measure, manage, and improve their piece of the process. An organization can develop a new system by incorporating the following five principles:

1. Let teams take the lead in designing the new system
2. Create process measures, not functional measures
3. Use only a few key measurements
4. Make sure that management does not use the new system to punish or control teams
5. Link together a balanced set of long-term and short-term performance and learning measures

Principle One: Let teams Take the Lead in Designing the New System

The natural work teams in the organization must play the lead role in developing the new performance measurement system. Since they are the ones doing the work, they are most capable of determining the type of measures they need to gauge their performance. This enables the teams to measure, manage, and improve their piece of the process without being dependent on management to point out areas that need improvement. A win-win situation is created as management saves time and natural work teams gain more control and ownership over their work.

If top management were to create the new performance measurement system working in isolation, they would undoubtedly develop a system geared toward management's information needs rather than the needs of the teams. This would force the teams to devote precious time to collecting and analyzing data that was of little use to them. It would also require them to spend extra time searching for measures that would give them feedback on their work.

To create an effective performance measurement system, an organization must use a joint development process. By using natural work team members as lead designers, individual teams can develop measures that will build in the feedback necessary for them to gauge their progress and improve their performance. From management's perspective, the measurement system should provide information on a few key measures that identify the performance of the company as a whole. By tracking a balanced set of key measures, management can assess the current financial state of the company as well as ensure that progress is being made throughout the company to maintain its competitive advantage.

As mentioned previously, the main goal of a measurement system is to detect performance improvements and deficits to determine the value being delivered to customers and to measure the financial wealth of the organization. Management needs to do more than simply identify problems or potential weaknesses or track financial performance. To continuously deliver value to customers, teams and management must take the necessary steps to correct the deficits and improve performance.

Principle Two: Create Process Measures, Not Functional Measures

Because your various natural work teams are designed to operate the core processes of the organization, you are ready to create a new measurement system based on process outcomes, not functional outcomes. In fact, if you designed your new organizational structure according to the recommendations in Chapter 8, there are no longer any functional silos in place for you have created a process-focused organization.

Process measures enable work teams to gauge their progress when the measures constantly indicate to the teams how well they are delivering value to their customers and adding to the bottom-line of the organization. The measures must be specific so that the team members can receive feedback that clearly shows them what aspects of their work is improving and where they need to focus their improvement efforts. Direct and immediate feedback from customers, both internal and external, is the best means by which team members can understand if they are truly delivering value to their customers. This fosters specific feedback as well as opens up communication channels, so an ongoing dialogue between the natural work teams and their customers becomes standard.

Feedback needs to be direct so that it pinpoints the specific behaviors that team members must change in order to improve their performance. For example, a statement from a team facilitator or coach informing his or her team of assembly line workers that quality levels are down does nothing to let the employees know what they each must do differently to improve quality. On the other hand, if the same facilitator informs his or her work team that a wiring problem is causing quality levels to drop on certain product-lines, and then demonstrates how to fix the problem by providing additional training, the employees are then capable of and willing to change their behavior and improve quality.

Immediate feedback is necessary because it allows team members to correct problems before the costs increase significantly, and more importantly, before the customers end up with the product or service containing the problem. For instance, a natural work team responsible for processing insurance claims benefits from receiving immediate feedback from the team responsible for adjusting claims. Weekly feedback would have little impact on the claims service representative's ability to deliver value to their internal customer, because they would have to rework a significant number of claims by the time the problem was finally brought to their attention. Even worse, the claims adjuster may overlook the problem because it is not his or her responsibility, and thus the final customers may be the ones who end up dealing with the problem.

Principle Three: Use Only a Few Key Measurements

Too large a number of measurements will shift a work team's focus from the customer, where it should be, to collecting data and monitoring activities. A handful of measurements can suffice in most situations, as a few measurements usually can give natural work teams enough feedback to determine their performance levels and track their progress.

Christopher Meyer, in his *Harvard Business Review* article, "How the Right Measures Help Teams Excel," discusses how the "what gets measured gets done" philosophy has led many companies to dramatically increase the number of measures they incorporate into their measurement system. His car dashboard analogy highlights how a simple and clear measurement system can help teams to eliminate many of the extra measurements that do nothing to help them excel:

> Trying to run a team without a good, simple guidance system is like trying to drive a car without a dashboard. We might do it in a pinch but not as a matter of practice, because

we'd lack the necessary information—the speed, the amount of fuel, the engine temperature—to ensure that we reach our destination.[2]

Natural work teams can use the following general guidelines to help them select measures that provide them with the necessary feedback without spending too much time gathering and analyzing information.

- Select four or five performance measures that will be customer-focused outcomes, not activities
- Each key area should have a measure
- Periodically review measures to determine if they need to be replaced by other more useful ones
- Share measures with other teams and when similar measures are identified, then the separate teams should consider becoming one larger team
- Do not measure anything that the natural work team cannot have significant influence over

If teams need help creating measures for their work, they should first try to meet with other teams that have successfully established effective performance measures. If you need to turn to management for help, they need to make sure that the measures remain focused on improving team performance. Used for any other purpose, measures become punitive.

Principle Four: Make Sure That Management Does Not Use the New System to Control Teams

By having the natural work teams be the lead developers of the new measurement system, you can usually prohibit management from installing measurements that can be used to control the teams. However, over time some "old school" managers, who have the old mentality of mistrusting employees, may manipulate the measurement system back to constantly monitoring the team's every move.

To truly empower the natural work teams throughout the organization, management must trust each and every one of its employees. Otherwise, management will eventually use the measurement system to control and monitor the activities of its employees, regressing to the old school thinking and undermining their organizational transformation effort.

In his article, "Control in the Age of Empowerment," Robert Simmons, Professor of Business Management at Harvard Business School, uses Nordstrom as an example of a company where management removed the control mechanisms that in turn gave their employees a wide latitude to deliver exceptional customer service. "To unleash this type of potential," he says, "senior managers must give up the control over many kinds of decisions and allow employees at lower levels of the organization to act independently. Good managers work constantly to help employees rise to their potential."[3]

Forcing employees to adhere to a rigid policy manual or seek authorization for day-to-day decision making runs counter to providing exceptional customer service. Customers, especially in the retail industry, value speed or service as much as quality and price. If you are new to the idea of empowerment, don't blindly give up control and stop measuring your employees. Instead, provide business, team, and customer service training, and work with your teams to develop measures that will help them track and improve their performance.

Letting go of control and intervening only when necessary are some of the new responsibilities of management in the newly transformed organization. The measurement system described in this chapter shifts the responsibility of monitoring performance from top management to the various natural work teams. This is appropriate because the teams that require information and feedback to improve performance should be the ones responsible for gathering it.

Surprisingly, even with the high awareness of employee involvement principles, there are still many archaic management ideas used to rule employees. Companies that cannot let go of control are incapable of establishing a culture based on trust. A computer software consultant once told me that his clients, the senior managers of a large regional bank, asked his firm to develop a measuring system for their new desktop software that would give management the ability to monitor the number of keystrokes bank employees were making on their computers at any given time. For instance, if 60 seconds passed with no activity the bank wanted the system to pinpoint the computer user who had failed to strike the keypad within the given time period.

With new technologies it is possible to find ever-increasing ways to monitor and control employee behavior. Going in this direction will negate any positive achievements realized during the transformation effort. It will destroy trust and switch management and employee focus to internal concerns. Management will be wasting time gathering useless data, i.e., number of keystrokes per employee per minute, while employees devote time to finding ways to avoid being caught. This is a negative path to travel down—a path to certain failure. To build trust throughout the organization, make all your measures public.

Principle 5: Link Together a Balanced Set of Long-Term and Short-Term Performance and Learning Measures

Equally important to natural work teams receiving the information and feedback they need to improve their performance, management needs long-term, strategic measures that reflect current performance and help predict future performance across the entire organization. By aligning and creating what is commonly called a *balanced scorecard*,[4] companies establish for all employees a link between their team activities and the company's overall performance. This has two primary benefits. One, by developing a system that links the performance of every team in the organization, senior management is able to quickly pull together all *scores* to accurately assess the company's overall business performance.

With the balanced scorecard, companies can measure their performance along four dimensions: 1) financial, 2) customer satisfaction, 3) internal business processes, and 4) learning and growth. This has many benefits. First, by focusing on more than just the financial aspect of the business the company can focus on the activities that will drive future performance, i.e., customer satisfaction and learning and growth. Additionally, by linking together the performance of all of the natural work teams in the organization, senior management is able to quickly pull together all scores to accurately assess the company's current business performance.

Equally, if not more important, with an aligned, linked, and balanced system, everyone is focused on their work team objectives and the company's strategic goals. This way, when a shift in strategic direction is deemed necessary, the already established measurement system serves as a communication pathway that aids in the development of new team objectives and performance targets, targets that are in line with the new or modified strategy.

In the absence of a clearly established method for keeping a balanced score throughout the company, organizations struggle with communicating and educating their employees on the performance and learning goals that are in place in all levels of the company. Also, if work teams do not know what numbers determine a win, they will have difficulty assessing their performance. This leads to confusion, especially when you ask teams to undertake performance improvement efforts. They simply will not know what to improve first or how to allocate their time or resources.

Individual Performance

Although the focus in this chapter has been on the development of a performance measurement system for natural work teams, it is important not to lose sight of the individual. Without individual performance there would be no team performance. Individual performance reviews are a necessary means by which individuals can receive comments on their personal development. Similar to work teams needing specific feedback to identify areas for improvement, individuals need ongoing feedback for their own personal development.

The focus of the performance review process should be on giving individual employees the feedback and assistance they need to improve their overall performance. This requires developing a personalized set of clear and measurable goals that reflect the individual's desire to increase his or her contribution to the team. Once the goals are set, individuals are then responsible for drafting a development plan to make the goals a reality. Some individuals may require assistance from their team leader and/or an internal consultant to develop their personal plan.

When it is time for individual performance reviews, employees should be assessed on 1) their contribution to their natural work team, 2) their work teams' overall success, and 3) the accomplishment of personal goals. Ideally, performance reviews are conducted by designated team members who also receive comments from other team members, the team leader, and internal and external customers. To maximize the effectiveness of the review, feedback should be specific, timely, and constructive. Whenever possible, give positive reinforcement. The performance review process is completed when the individual, with the assistance of the team review panel, develops a new set of goals for the upcoming period.

By ending the review process with the identification of goals and a development plan to achieve them, the review process begins and ends with a focus on continuous improvement. This performance review process, when operating effectively and performed regularly, maximizes the contribution of each individual in the organization. Tapping into the potential of all employees during the transformation effort helps the ongoing development of all employees. You can sustain this development process through an effective performance review process, a process that in turn will enhance your efforts to create a competitive advantage.

Chapter 10 illustrates the importance of providing work teams and individuals with the financial incentives that were previously reserved for management ranks only. If you do not have this last element in place, you will not truly empower your employees and your teams will not be motivated to make the leaps in performance you need to sustain a competitive advantage.

Create a Performance-Based Compensation System | **10**

> *"Effective incentive pay plans serve to link the employee (teams) to the economic fortunes of the organization in clear and meaningful ways."*
>
> —Thomas B. Wilson[1]

The organizational transformation model presented in the previous chapters has detailed all the major changes — culture, structure, processes, and so on. These are changes you must undertake to successfully transform an organization from a traditional, vertical organization, with all of its shortcomings, to a leaner, faster, and more flexible one. The last step needed to complete the transformation process is the redesign of the compensation system. Because work teams are the primary building blocks of performance in the newly transformed organization, it is important you redesign and link the compensation system with team performance.

How should the new compensation system look? Should you base the new system solely on team performance, or should the compensation system rely on a combination of individual, company, and team performance measures? How frequently should the rewards, i.e., compensation, be dispersed to sufficiently motivate employees? What non-monetary rewards are companies using to recognize and retain their employees?

Traditional Compensation Rewards
Lone-Ranger Behaviors

Traditional compensation systems were built for traditional organizations, compensating employees for individual work and rewarding managers for movement up the career ladder. As organizations transform into lean, market competitors, it is no wonder they find that the compensation systems of the past do not sufficiently recognize, reward, and retain employees for the future.

One of the main reasons why traditional compensation systems fail to align with newly transformed organizations is that they do not reward and recognize teamwork. In fact, traditional compensation systems commonly discourage teamwork, because yearly raises and bonuses are usually a fixed sum of money that is divided among the organization's members. Under this system individuals are forced to compete against each other, rather than help each other, to increase their yearly salary increase. "Traditional compensation reinforces lone-ranger behaviors and grandstanding as opposed to teamwork" says Edward W. Morse, in his *Performance Management Magazine* article, "Pay for Performance as Pie Comp: The Case for Contingent Compensation." "How else will one distinguish one's self from the rest of the team and thereby hope to garner a bigger slice of the pie?"[2]

Traditional compensation systems fail in other ways because they do not provide employees with the motivation they need to help them reach their performance objectives. Unlike managers and executives who are motivated to perform at higher levels because their incentives are structured according to the impact or control they have in their area, i.e., bonuses based on new business generated, frontline employees are rarely able to influence the amount of their bonuses or rewards. Even if bonuses are issued to employees, they are usually distributed in a lump sum at year end, with little or no connection made between performance and the reward. The employees will simply see it as a "Christmas" bonus—where every employee is treated the same.

Develop a Performance-Based Compensation System That Rewards and Motivates

Unlike traditional, bureaucratic organizations where jobs were purposely narrow and tasks relatively simple and repetitive, in newly transformed organizations employees are responsible for managing their performance, improving their work, working with customers, learning new skills, and developing new capabilities. With these new-found responsibilities there must follow a performance-based compensation system that motivates and rewards performance across all of these areas—a compensation system that recognizes, rewards, and retains employees.

Developing a new compensation system is a significant undertaking, but it is a necessary last step in completing the transformation of an organization. It is this step that provides all employees with the motivation to continuously learn, improve, and perform to their fullest potential. An organization that has been undergoing a transformation but then suddenly stops short by failing to redesign the compensation system is like a marathon runner quitting at the 25th mile.

The new system should be simple and easy to understand and administer. It should reinforce the goals of the organization and be economically and legally sound. Most importantly, compensation should be linked to individual, team, and company performance. To create this type of system you should incorporate the following five principles into your new design:

1. Use compensation teams to create the new system
2. Create a proper mix of individual, team, and business unit performance measures
3. Share results to motivate and reward teams that deliver value to their customers
4. Place no caps on the teams' bonuses or rewards
5. Disperse bonuses and/or rewards, and non-monetary accolades, frequently

Principle One: Use Compensation Teams to Create the New System

To establish a proper mix of individual, team, and business unit performance measures for the new compensation system, you should form a compensation team made up of a cross section of organizational members. Similar to transition teams redesigning processes and the organizational structure, a compensation team can readily develop a performance-based compensation system that aligns and links with the systems and structures already in place within the organization.

Compensation teams are successful when management and employees work together to develop a system that is both economically and legally sound, and that motivates and rewards all employees. Neither group working in isolation could develop a system that meets the above requirements. Management needs information from employees regarding what is sufficient motivation, while employees need help with economic and legal considerations.

Principle Two: Create a Proper Mix of Individual, Team, and Business Unit Performance Measures

A new compensation system must account for the individuals in the organization. Too much emphasis on natural work teams or company performance can overshadow the work done by the individuals inside the teams and throughout the organization. There is no standard (or perfect) formula you can use to determine the individual, team, and company performance results ratio. An appropriate mix is usually determined by the degree of interdependency existing between the individual team members and the different teams in the organization.

As a rule, when there is a high degree of interdependency between members of the teams and among the teams themselves, then team and company performance should determine a large percentage of the bonuses that are paid out. Conversely, when teams are mostly autonomous and team members have other responsibilities outside of their immediate team, compensation should be based mostly on a mixture of individual and team performance. In all cases I recommend that some percentage of compensation be based in all three areas. Even if the percentage of compensation reflected from company or business unit performance is a token amount or results in no money being distributed, a three-prong compensation system helps employees to stay focused on the overall goals and objectives of the company.

This mix of individual, natural work team, and company or business unit performance should be directly aligned with the balanced scorecard system discussed in the previous chapter. It recognizes and rewards individuals for learning new skills and developing new capabilities as measured against their personal development plan. It reinforces teamwork through incentives and motivates teams throughout the organization to find new ways to improve performance. Lastly, it links together the efforts and achievements of everyone in the organization into an overall dollar value that is shared with employees.

Principle Three: Share Results to Motivate and Reward Teams That Deliver Value to Their Customers

The central aspect of the new compensation system must be to reward those natural work teams that deliver value to their customers. Whether it be to internal or external customers, you can measure value-delivery by determining the degree by which the various teams accomplished or exceeded their performance objectives. Rewarding those teams that deliver added value to their customers benefits everyone in the organization.

Edward Lawler, Professor of Management and Organization in the Graduate School of Business Administration at the University of Southern California, discusses in his book, *The Ultimate Advantage: Creating the High-Involvement Organization,* the dangers that can result from not sharing financial rewards with employees:

> When, as a result of employees efforts, organizational performance improves, employees expect to share in the gains. If they do not share in the gains, they feel exploited and ultimately reject management systems that give them more information, knowledge, and power and ask them for better performance but do not reward them for their performance.[3]

When you properly design a new compensation system, you can create a win-win situation for all organizational members—one in which the organization only rewards work teams when they deliver a certain level (or greater) of value to their customers. By designing the system this way, the organization ensures itself that any financial reward payouts are only a percentage of the extra profit the teams bring in. Increasing the value delivered to the customers, the profit received by the company, and the rewards distributed to the team members are certainly compelling reasons why top management should give teams financial incentives.

PRATT & WHITNEY. This is but one company that has realized the benefits of sharing results with their employees. Faced with rising costs and decreased demand for military planes after the end of the Cold War, the company's jet-engine parts plant factory in North Berwick, Maine almost closed in 1993. In a major effort to cut costs the company created a *results-sharing plan* through the combined effort of management and frontline employees. This is a plan that delivers bonuses to hourly and salaried employees based on the achievement of performance targets. The results-sharing plan, along with other initiatives, has been so successful that the North Berwick plant has not only survived, but is planning to add jobs.

As Joseph B. White wrote in his *Wall Street Journal* article, "Dodging Doom: How a Creaky Factory Got Off the Hit List (and) Won Respect at Last," "Pratt used financial carrots rather than just sticks to persuade employees to adopt cost-saving new work techniques."[4] These carrots have motivated everyone in the organization to find opportunities to cut costs and improve performance. These cost-savings have not only helped to secure jobs, but have resulted in payouts of over $1,500 per shopfloor employee in the first year.[5]

Principle Four: Place No Caps on the Teams' Bonuses or Rewards

As long as the teams deliver value to customers, and thus profits to the company, the teams should continue to share a certain percentage of the additional revenues resulting from their performance improvement. This is not to say that companies cannot, and should not, raise the performance levels they desire from the teams. If this does occur, companies should consider providing their teams with a larger percentage of the profits as they make it more difficult for the teams to obtain their yearly objectives. Simply putting caps on the size of their bonus or reward can undermine the whole purpose of the compensation system.

The compensation system Rockwell International put in place in their Tactical Systems Division incorporated many of the elements previously mentioned. Namely, top management did not place a cap on the amount of money employees could receive from the new gainsharing plan. The system measures specific quality indicators that allows rewards to be distributed to the teams that have accomplished their objectives. Furthermore, when Rockwell International raises performance standards, as they do every year, the payout ratio increases in favor of the employees. As Rockwell International shows, continuously developing new financial "carrots" motivates your teams to improve performance and in turn generates greater profit for your company.

In 1987, for instance, 80 percent of the additional savings the teams generated—or profits they were responsible for increasing—went to the company, and 20 percent went to the employees of the teams. Currently the performance standards are much higher, but the payout ratio has increased in favor of the employees. The present ratio is approximately 65 percent to the company and 35 percent to the teams.[6] Though it may be harder for the teams to find cost-cutting opportunities, they are receiving a higher percentage of each dollar they save or additional profits they bring in.

Principle Five: Disperse Bonuses and/or Rewards, and Non-Monetary Accolades, Frequently

Effective bonus or reward/recognition systems link high levels of performance with immediate financial payouts as often as possible. A compensation system can pay out a high percentage to the teams coupled with other types of positive reinforcement, but without frequent distribution of rewards, the compensation system may not be motivating to the teams. Teams must see how changing their behavior can influence their near-term and long-term financial situation in a positive way.

In general, you should distribute bonuses to employees or teams soon after they meet their desired performance objectives. The frequency of the payouts will depend on the nature of the organization designing the new compensation system. If product completion or service delivery is complex and requires several months, organizations may be forced to pay out bonuses semiannually or even yearly. To link performance with compensation more closely, organizations in these situations might consider adopting a plan that allows team members to see how much they are increasing their bonus, on a monthly or quarterly basis, but then saves the actual financial payout for when the product is completed or the service delivered.

It is important for individuals and natural work teams to understand up front how frequently the organization will be distributing rewards or recognition. To aid in this understanding, some organizations have created recognition charts that

Table 10-1. Reward and Recognition Chart

Individual reward or recognition for:	Frequency	Team reward or recognition for:	Frequency
Sharing knowledge	Randomly	Achieving team goals	Monthly & Annually
Exceptional contribution to the team	Randomly	Transfer of knowledge between teams	Randomly
Advanced skill learning	Monthly	Becoming more self-managed	Randomly
Customer recognition of good performance	Randomly	Increasing team profitability	Monthly
Exceptional work	Monthly	Customer recognition of good performance	Randomly
Innovative thinking	Randomly	Coming in under budget	Quarterly & Annually
Achievement of individual goals	Annually	Ongoing process improvement	Randomly
Volunteer work (company or community	Randomly	Smart risk taking (successful or not)	Randomly

show how often rewards and recognition will occur. Table 10-1 is such a chart.

These principles provide a framework on which you can build a new performance-based compensation system that motivates and rewards all employees for achieving or surpassing their performance goals. The next section stresses the importance of non-monetary instruments to attract and retain employees.

Beyond Money: Nonmonetary Instruments to Retain Employees

Companies in virtually every industry are developing innovative ways to reduce turnover and retain their employees. In the past, salary increases, bonuses, and rapid progression up the career ladder were mostly sufficient in maintaining employee loyalty. Yes, some valuable employees were lost to competitors who offered more job responsibility and variety as well as a higher quality of work life, but few companies thought that kind of stuff was important. This has all changed.

What has changed? In a word, everything. The aging workforce combined with the premium placed on intelligence has created a shortage in knowledge work industries. Coupled with the skyrocketing costs of worker turnover, due to the amount of time and money invested in training employees, companies are reconsidering ways to attract and retain their workforce. This is all happening at the same time that employees are struggling to find new ways to balance family and work life, due in part to the steady increase in the number of dual-income households. For these types of employees, time is becoming more valuable than money.

What are companies doing to counter these trends? Progressive organizations are going beyond simply offering flexible work hours (flextime) to attract and retain employees. They are developing in-house services and policies that increase the quality of work and personal life for their employees. From sending a concierge to your house to wait for the plumber (Andersen Consulting) to encouraging telecommuting (AT&T), organizations are beginning to realize that employees are seeking out and staying with companies that understand their professional and personal needs.

Family-Friendly Workplaces

By considering the "whole" employee, i.e., their personal and professional responsibilities, employers are able to customize their workplace to create a diverse range of work opportunities and services to employees demanding more than the traditional

9–5 job with a paycheck at the end of the month. "To put it somewhat differently," says Kerry A. Dolan in her *Forbes* article, "When Money Isn't Enough," "workers want the workplace to take on some of the attributes of family life. This is especially true with today's younger workers."[7]

Family-friendly workplaces, as they are often called, contribute to lower turnover rates and create more productive organizations. According to the National Commission for Employment Policy, parents who have their children in on-site child care centers are more productive, take less leave time, and have better attitudes toward work. Our corporations, communities, and nation will benefit from the creation of workplaces that make family life and work life not a trade-off, but a joint effort.

A good way to start creating a workplace that embraces the move toward a higher quality of work life is by using an employee survey that identifies employee needs and wants. Similar to developing a new compensation system that will sufficiently motivate employees, employees should play a major role in creating this new, more worker friendly environment. Be aware of your employees needs. Providing a child care center or on-site public school will not significantly decrease employee turnover if large numbers of your workers are single or married without children. Find out what employees want the most and have a team of managers and employees work together to make the workplace a desirable place to work.

Chapter 11 discusses how organizations must provide all employees with the opportunity to continuously learn if they wish to sustain their competitive advantage. As I have stressed throughout this book, employees cannot continually improve their performance unless companies are dedicated to providing ongoing learning opportunities.

Make Learning Available to All Employees 11

> *"The person who figures out how to harness the collective genius of the people in his or her organization is going to blow the competition away."*
>
> — WALTER WRISTON[1]
> (FORMER CEO OF CITIBANK)

An organizational transformation is never truly complete. Rather, it is series of large-scale changes—to the culture, processes, structure, and so on—over the course of a given time period, approximately one to three years, followed by continuous learning and ongoing improvement by all employees. Eventually, despite such improvement efforts, industry conditions and/or technological developments will necessitate another transformation in the years ahead.

To maximize the effectiveness and prolong the gains realized from the transformation, organizations must make learning available to all employees. Without ongoing learning, employees and the organization become stagnant and the need for a large-scale turnaround quickly becomes a reality once again. This wastes company resources and creates an environment with little stability and few opportunities to learn new skills.

Individuals can only sustain drastic periods of change, such as a transformation effort, for a short time. Employees need periods of prolonged stability in the workplace, otherwise they will seek opportunities elsewhere that allow them to learn and improve in a safer and less stressful environment. A continuous learning and improvement culture, as outlined in this chapter, provide employees with the training and time they need to safely learn new skills and develop new competencies.

Employees Must Learn How to Manage Their Career Growth

How do you go about making learning available for all employees? You must first empower individuals and natural work teams to take responsibility for identifying the particular skill areas they need to develop or improve. Management should assist individuals and teams with skill assessments as well as personal and team development plans, but they should not be responsible for managing and monitoring every individual's skill development. Employees must learn how to manage their own career growth. They must understand that their career growth and success will be based on their ability to learn new skills, gain experience in different areas of the company, and transfer their knowledge to others. Companies must also have financial incentives in place to motivate employees to make the effort to learn. In this way there is a commitment on both parties to improve individual and company performance.

Natural work teams must also clearly understand the vision and strategic direction of the company in order for team members to learn new skills; then the team can make performance improvements that are consistent with the overall goals and objectives of the organization. This is especially true when work teams are responsible for redesigning systems to support or enhance the core processes of the organization. The following example highlights this point.

After the transformation effort at The Union Pacific Railroad, the company created Quality Improvement Teams (QITs) to improve processes that were bypassed during their reengineering phase. Because these support processes were not critical aspects of the core value-delivery process at the railroad, plans were made to redesign them at a later stage so as not to prolong the reengineering phase. The first process a QIT was responsible for redesigning was the internal telephone call transfer system. By understanding the objectives of the organization—to deliver the information to those who need it the most—the assigned team was able to develop a new call transfer process that helped to facilitate the delivery of needed information to the customers, frontline employees, and top management.[2]

Without a clear understanding of the company's objectives regarding information flow, this team may have wrongly assumed that top managers need to preview all important information before it is delivered to the work teams. But because the company clearly communicated the vision and objectives to the improvement teams no such mishap occurred—information flows unrestricted to those that need it for decision-making purposes.

Clearly small process redesign efforts do not radically improve company performance like what occurs during an organizational transformation, when dramatic improvements are expected from radical changes to the way work gets done. These small process redesign efforts are consistent with the goals of continuous improvement—realizing incremental improvements in quality, service, cost, and speed. It is when the improvement efforts of all employees and teams are combined that a company realizes significant gains, gains that dramatically improve your efforts in sustaining a competitive advantage.

Learning Organizations

Continuous improvement must become part of an organization's culture, whereby every employee looks to improve his or her performance. Without a shared commitment to improving performance, the efforts made by some will be negated by others who are comfortable with the status quo. A shared dissatisfaction with the status quo leads to the creation of continuous learning and improvement as a cultural norm.

To develop this type of culture, individuals must work with their teammates, team leaders, and coaches to develop personal development plans as described in Chapter 9. After this step, natural team members must reinforce each other if any progress is going to be made toward the completion of their goals. Learning new skills and changing behaviors is not as difficult when you have support and assistance from colleagues. And when everyone is in it together, learning can even become fun.

Organizations can formally support learning for all employees by creating what is frequently called *learning organizations*. In learning organizations, management goes beyond providing some training classes or educational assistance, to the establishment of a system by which all employees can continuously learn. It can be a company university as the case of Motorola University. Or as at 3M, you can ask employees to spend time during each work week on innovative projects that spark learning. Whatever approach you take, formal systems help place learning within reach of everyone.

Within these formal systems employees are encouraged to challenge existing approaches, approaches that will assist them in attaining the company's vision and objectives. You can create the kind of environment where employees are taught how to learn. Instead of being afraid to make mistakes, employees will feel freer to experiment. "Unfortunately, " says Peter M. Senge, author of *The Leader's New Work: Creating Learning Organizations*, "the primary institutions of our society are oriented predominantly toward controlling rather than learning, rewarding individuals for performing for others rather than for cultivating their natural curiosity and impulse to learn."[3]

When a company creates a formal learning system their employees no longer have to navigate the corporate walls in search of learning opportunities. Training classes, off-site learning opportunities, and other types of educational assistance are communicated throughout the organization and made accessible to everyone. This proactive approach to organizational learning pays off as all employees can develop the new skills they need to increase their performance.

On-Line Learning Systems

Some companies are developing formal learning opportunities for all of their employees through the use of on-line learning systems. There is one client I worked with who created a computer-based learning system allowing every employee to access the system to search and retrieve information. Subjects ranged from better communication to planned risk taking to sharing information with colleagues. Internal and external training sessions are posted on the system and updated on a regular basis. The e-mail addresses of specialists or experts are listed in many skill categories, allowing employees to contact these individuals for further material or one-on-one information sharing. They continually update the system to give frequent users new and valuable information. To better understand employees' changing needs they use surveys to measure the strengths and weaknesses of the system and to identify areas for improvement. Lastly, employees are expected to use the system on company time and encouraged to work with other employees and their coaches to develop their skills.

Employees who fail to take advantage of a formal learning system weaken the learning culture and slow down the rate at which the company can continuously improve. Companies need to establish consequences to ensure that these employees are motivated to learn new skills. If employees still resist taking advantage of the company's learning opportunities and their performance remains stagnant or drops, you must remove them from the company. Otherwise the organization jeopardizes its ability to add more value to customers, hindering its ability to maintain a competitive advantage.

Everyone Wins in a Continuously Learning Culture

By installing a formal learning system employees can continually learn; only when employees continually learn can they continually improve. But for a continuous improvement culture to become a reality, they need a performance-based compensation system to motivate and reward them. For companies that establish such a culture, everyone wins. Customers receive more value through lower prices, higher quality products and services, and faster turnaround times. Employees and management will share a percentage of the higher profits they helped achieve and secure their employment as the organization's market share increases. Lastly, shareholders will realize greater returns as the company increases its overall net worth and as greater numbers of investors try to buy into the company's current and predicted future success.

It Takes Good Planning and Great Execution | **12**

"An organizational transformation is (most often) successful when there is good planning and great execution. Unfortunately, most businesses fail to do anything with the strategy they create."

— HARRY MOSER[1]
(GEMINI CONSULTING)

The organizational transformation plan contained in this book is unique in that it addresses all of the components that affect organizational performance. From changing the corporate culture to redesigning core processes to creating a new performance measurement system, this comprehensive strategic change plan enables organizations to dramatically improve customer satisfaction, employee performance, and investor return.

What is not unique about this transformation plan, nor any other change methodology, is that for it to really work there must be great execution. A partial commitment to change the organization on the part of management will not create a competitive advantage. Likewise, a terrific redesign on paper that never gets fully implemented will fail to bring about significant and lasting change.

What brings about significant and lasting change is strong leadership, commitment, trust, and a transformation plan that works. This plan works because it considers the whole organization from the beginning rather than from pieces to be assembled at the end. It starts with challenging leaders to embrace change, to form a new strategic direction and vision, and to build a new company culture. It then outlines a change management plan that stresses communication and develops a road map so that employees can understand how the company plans to attain its new vision. The plan then emphasizes the need to tap into the potential of all employees and details the role employees should play in designing the future organization.

With employees and management co-leading the transformation, the plan moves to the redesign of the company's core business processes. This stage is completed when the new processes are aligned and linked to form a network of capabilities that create a competitive advantage. With the new processes in place, the transformation plan details the steps needed to install natural work teams as the means by which work will be accomplished. Following the establishment of the work teams, the plan focuses on the need to rebuild the rest of the organizational structure — middle and senior management positions. After the structure has been rebuilt, the transformation plan switches to the creation of a performance measurement system that delivers feedback to the teams and individuals who need it to improve their performance.

After you complete all of the above stages, the plan calls for a new performance-based compensation system that motivates employees and rewards them for the attainment of performance goals. By then making learning and improvement available to all employees, the transformation plan ends with the creation of a continuous learning and improvement culture thus sustaining the company's competitive advantage.

The plan also works because it is relatively simple and easy to follow. The new culture taps into the potential of all employees. Redesigned processes dramatically improve company performance and customer satisfaction. The new structure provides the teams with the support they need to handle the day-to-day aspects of the business, freeing up management to focus on business growth and other strategic issues. The measurement system identifies individuals and natural work teams who achieve their performance goals, while the compensation system rewards them for it. The learning and improvement culture sustains the company's competitive advantage for several years until business conditions change and technologies unveil new business opportunities or threats that necessitate another transformation.

Organizational transformation is not easy. The path to a successful transformation is often met with many obstacles. You will be confronted with people who doubt your plans and resist your every move. Do not fight your resistors. Rather, help educate those who do not yet understand the value of transforming the workplace, who have yet to tap into the potential of all employees. Be patient, stay focused, and do not lose hope. Your perseverance and dedication will pay off as your organization succeeds.

Reference Notes

Chapter 1

1. James Burke, quoted in *21st Century Leadership*, by Lynne Joy McFarland, Larry E. Senn, and John R. Childress (Los Angeles, CA: The Leadership Press, 1993), p. 51.
2. Research interview, 1994.
3. Noel M. Tichy and Stratford Sherman, *Control Your Destiny or Someone Else Will: Lessons in Mastering Change—The Principles Jack Welch Is Using to Revolutionize General Electric* (New York, NY: HarperCollins, 1993, 1994), p. xxiii.

Chapter 2

1. James O'Toole, *Leading Change: Overcoming the Ideology of Comfort and the Tyranny of Custom* (San Francisco, CA: Jossey-Bass, 1995).
2. Bernard M. Bass, "From Transactional to Transformational Leadership: Learning to Share the Vision," *Organizational Dynamics,* vol. 18, no. 3, Winter 1990, p. 21.
3. Ibid, p. 22
4. Michael Porter, "What is Strategy?" *Harvard Business Review*, Nov.–Dec. 1996, p. 70.
5. John Case, *Open-Book Management: The Coming Business Revolution* (New York, NY: HarperCollins, 1995), p. 37.
6. Research interview, 1995.
7. Noel M. Tichy and Stratford Sherman, *Control Your Destiny or Someone Else Will: Lessons in Mastering Change—The Principles Jack Welch Is Using to Revolutionize General Electric* (New York, NY: HarperCollins, 1994), p. 4.
8. Connie Brittain, "Reengineering Complements BellSouth's Major Business Strategies," *Industrial Engineering,* February 1994, p. 35.
9. Research interview, 1994.
10. John H. Zenger, Ed Musselwhite, Kathleen Hurson, and Craig Perrin, *Leading Teams: Mastering the New Role* (Homewood, Illinois: Business One Irwin, 1994), p. 37.
11. Research interview, 1994. Hagood Bellinger, Executive-in-Residence, Graduate School of Management, Georgia Institute of Technology.
12. Noel M. Tichy and Stratford Sherman, *Control Your Destiny or Someone Else Will: Lessons in Mastering Change—The Principles Jack Welch Is Using to Revolutionize General Electric* (New York, NY: HarperCollins, 1993, 1994), p. 299.
13. Peter M. Senge, "The Leader's New Work: Building Learning Organizations," *Sloan Management Review*, Fall 1990, p. 7.

Chapter 3

1. James O'Toole, *Leading Change: Overcoming the Ideology of Comfort and the Tyranny of Custom* (San Francisco, CA: Jossey-Bass, 1995), p. 37.
2. Ibid, p. 15.
3. Research interview, 1995.
4. J. Richard Hackman, "Can Empowerment Work at SportsGear?" *Harvard Business Review*, January–February 1995, p. 26.
5. Gary Hamel and C. K. Prahalad, *Competing for the Future: Breakthrough Strategies for Seizing Control of Your Industry and Creating the Market of Tomorrow* (Boston, MA: Harvard Business School Press, 1994), p. 22.
6. Research interview, 1994.
7. Lawrence M. Miller, with Helene Uhlfelder, Ph.D., Duane Cross, John Burden, and Ron Robinson, *Whole Systems Architecture—Beyond Reengineering: Designing the High-Performance Organization* (Atlanta, GA: Miller Howard Consulting Group, Inc.), p. 49.
8. James A. Belasco, "This Vision Thing," *Executive Excellence*, January 1990, p. 3.
9. Edgar H. Schein, Working paper: "How Can Organizations Learn Faster? The Problem of Entering the Green Room," April 1992.
10. Ibid.
11. Jeanie Daniel Duck, "Managing Change: The Art of Balancing," *Harvard Business Review*, November–December 1993, p. 111.

Chapter 4

1. J. Richard Hackman, "Can Empowerment Work at SportsGear?", *Harvard Business Review*, January–February 1995, p. 26.
2. Ralph Stayer, "How I Learned to Let My Workers Lead," *Harvard Business Review*, November–December 1990, p. 68.
3. Edward E. Lawler, III, *The Ultimate Advantage: Creating the High Involvement Organization* (San Francisco, CA: Jossey-Bass, 1994), p. 57.
4. James C. Collins and Jerry I. Porras, *Built to Last: Successful Habits of Visionary Companies* (New York, NY: HarperCollins, 1994), p. 117.
5. United States Department of Labor, "High Performance Work Practices and Firm Performance," August 1993.
6. Casey Ichniowski, Kathryn Shaw, and Giovanna Prennushi, "Effects of Human Resource Management Practices on Productivity," Columbia University, June 10, 1993.
7. Ann Bartel, "Productivity Gains from the Implementation of Employee Training Programs," *Industrial Relations*, in press.
8. David I. Levine and Laura D'Andrea Tyson, "Participation, Productivity, and the Firm's Environment" in *Paying for Productivity*, ed. by Alan Blinder. (Washington, DC: The Brookings Institution, 1990), pp. 183–235.

Chapter 5

1. Research interview, February 1995.
2. Robert Eaton, quoted in "Empowerment That Pays Off," *Fortune*, March 20, 1995, pp. 145–46.

3. Linda M. Bradshaw, "PICOS: Focusing on Customer Satisfaction," General Motors Internal Document, 1994, p. 2.
4. "From the Past to the Future—The PICOS Project: A Modern Process Improvement Technique," *Hospital Management*, April 1996, p. 7.

Chapter 6

1. Michael Hammer and James Champy, *Reengineering the Corporation* (New York, NY: HarperCollins, 1971), p. 41.
2. Ibid, pp. 42–43.
3. Thomas Davenport, quoted in "Reengineering—The Hot New Managing Tool," *Fortune*, August 23, 1993, p. 42.
4. Research interview, February 1995.
5. John Hagel, "Keeping Core Process Redesign (CPR) on Track, *The McKinsey Quarterly,* 1993, no. 1, p. 65.
6. Gene Hall, Jim Rosenthal, and Judy Wade, "How to Make Reengineering Really Work," *Harvard Business Review*, November–December 1993, p. 128.
7. John Hagel, "Keeping Core Process Redesign (CPR) on Track, *The McKinsey Quarterly,* 1993, no. 1, p. 65.
8. Gene Hall, Jim Rosenthal, and Judy Wade, "How to Make Reengineering Really Work," *Harvard Business Review*, November–December 1993, p. 122.
9. Rod Laird, quoted in John Browning's article "The Power of Process Redesign," *The McKinsey Quarterly*, 1993, no. 1, p. 55.
10. Ibid, p. 125.
11. Karl Newkirk, quoted in John J. Xenakis's article "Taming SAP," *CIO*, 1996, p. 23.
12. United States Department of Labor, *High Performance Work Practices and Firm Performance*, August 1993.
13. Research interview, November 1994.
14. Presentation by Young, Clark & Associates, November 1995.
15. Ibid.

Chapter 7

1. Edward E. Lawler, *The Ultimate Advantage: Creating the High-Involvement Organization* (San Francisco, CA: Jossey-Bass, 1992), p. 28.
2. Research interview, November 1994.
3. Andrew Kupfer, "An Outsider Fires Up a Railroad," *Fortune*, December 18, 1989, p. 142.
4. Research interview, March 1995.
5. John Zenger, Ed Musselwhite, Kathleen Hurson, and Craig Perrin, *Leading Teams: Mastering the New Role* (Homewood, Illinois: Business One Irwin, 1994), p. 94.
6. Burnes P. Hollyman and Robert L. Howie, "Chase Manhattan: Banking Hard Dollar Paybacks from ITR," in "Mastering Change: Information Technology Integration in Successful Enterprises," a special advertising feature in *Business Week*, December 19, 1994.
7. J. Richard Hackman, "Why This Team Doesn't Work," *Harvard Business Review*, November–December, 1994. p. 30.

Chapter 8

1. Margaret Wheatley and Myron Kellner-Rogers, "Self-Organization: The Irresistible Future of Organizing," *Strategy & Leadership*, July/August 1996, p. 23.
2. Research interview, November 1994.
3. Research interview, November 1994.
4. Research interview, May 1994.
5. David Halberstam, *The Reckoning* (New York, NY: Avon Books, 1986), pp. 243–246.

Chapter 9

1. Christopher Meyer, "How the Right Measures Help Teams Excel," *Harvard Business Review*, May–June 1994, p. 96.
2. Ibid, p. 96.
3. Robert Simmons, "Control in the Age of Empowerment," *Harvard Business Review*, March–April 1995, p. 88.
4. Robert S. Kaplan and David P. Norton, "The Balanced Scorecard— Measures That Drive Performance," *Harvard Business Review*, January–February, 1992, p. 71.

Chapter 10

1. Thomas B. Wilson, "Changing the Purpose of Pay Programs," *Performance Management Magazine*, volume 9, no. 2, p. 30.
2. Edward W. Morse, "'Pay for Performance as Pie Comp: The Case for Contingent Compensation," *Performance Management Magazine*, vol. 6, no. 2, p. 23.
3. Edward E. Lawler III, *The Ultimate Advantage: Creating the High-Involvement Organization* (San Francisco, CA: Jossey-Bass, 1992), pp. 172–73.
4. Joseph B. White, "Dodging Doom: How a Creaky Factory Got Off the Hit List (and) Won Respect at Last," *The Wall Street Journal*, December 26, 1996, column 6, p. 1.
5. Ibid.
6. Research interview, November 1994.
7. Kerry A. Dolan, "When Money Isn't Enough," *Forbes*, November 18, 1996, p. 167.

Chapter 11

1. Walter Wriston, former Citibank CEO, quoted in Peter M. Senge's, "The Leader's New Work: Building Learning Organizations," *Sloan Management Review*, Fall 1990, pp. 7–8.
2. Tom Peters, *Liberation Management*, (New York, NY: Random House, 1992), p. 96.
3. Peter M. Senge, "The Leader's New Work: Building Learning Organizations," *Sloan Management Review*, Fall 1990, p. 7.

Chapter 12

1. Research interview, 1995.

About the Author

Christopher W. Head is a consultant and knowledge manager with Miller Howard Consulting Group in Atlanta, Georgia. He received his Master of Science in Management from Georgia Institute of Technology in Atlanta.

Christopher began this book as a graduate student at Georgia Tech, where he conducted field research with BellSouth, Rockwell International, Southland Life, DeKalb Medical Center, and The Southern Company. He conducted additional research with several management consulting firms, including Gemini Consulting, Deloitte & Touche, Andersen Consulting, and Ernst & Young.

Since joining Miller Howard Consulting Group he has assisted with the transformation efforts of several organizations. He also co-developed and manages an Internet-based on-line consulting, research, and electronic library service titled, "The Change Management Knowledge Center." His specific business interests include change management and leadership development, as well as the transformation of the healthcare industry. Learn more about the author by visiting http://www.millerhoward.com on the World Wide Web or send e-mail to chrishead@mindspring.com.

Subject Index

Books from Productivity Press

Productivity Press publishes books that empower individuals and companies to achieve excellence in quality, productivity, and the creative involvement of all employees. Through steadfast efforts to support the vision and strategy of continuous improvement, Productivity Press delivers today's leading-edge tools and techniques gathered directly from industry leaders around the world. Call toll-free (800) 394-6868 for our free catalog.

TO ORDER: Write, phone, or fax Productivity Press, Dept. BK, P.O. Box 13390, Portland, OR 97213-0390, phone 1-800-394-6868, fax 1-800-394-6286.

Outside the U.S. phone (503) 235-0600; fax (503) 235-0909

Send check or charge to your credit card (American Express, Visa, Master-Card accepted).

U.S. ORDERS: Add $5 shipping for first book, $2 each additional for UPS surface delivery. Add $5 for each AV program containing 1 or 2 tapes; add $12 for each AV program containing 3 or more tapes. We offer attractive quantity discounts for bulk purchases of individual titles; call for more information.

ORDER BY E-MAIL: Order 24 hours a day from anywhere in the world. Use either address:

To order: **service@ppress.com**
To view the online catalog and/or order: **http://www.ppress.com/**

QUANTITY DISCOUNTS: For information on quantity discounts, please contact our sales department.

INTERNATIONAL ORDERS: Write, phone, or fax for quote and indicate shipping method desired. For international callers, telephone number is 503-235-0600 and fax number is 503-235-0909. Prepayment in U.S. dollars must accompany your order (checks must be drawn on U.S. banks). When quote is returned with payment, your order will be shipped promptly by the method requested.

NOTE: Prices are in U.S. dollars and are subject to change without notice.